W9-ACQ-538

Easy CRYSTAL STITCHING
Sophisticated Jewelry

NIKIA ANGEL

KB
KALMBACH BOOKS

Kalmbach Books
21027 Crossroads Circle
Waukesha, Wisconsin 53186
www.Kalmbach.com/Books

© 2012 by Nikia Angel
All rights reserved. Except for brief excerpts for review, this book may not be
reproduced in part or in whole by electronic means or otherwise without written
permission of the publisher.

Illustrations by the author. Photography by Kalmbach Books.

The designs in *Easy Crystal Stitching—Sophisticated Jewelry* are the copyrighted
property of the author and they may not be taught or sold without permission.
Please use them for your education and personal enjoyment only.

Published in 2012
16 15 14 13 12   1 2 3 4 5

Manufactured in the United States of America

ISBN: 978-0-87116-439-1
EISBN: 978-0-87116-735-4

Editor: Erica Swanson
Technical Editor: Jane Danley Cruz
Art Director: Lisa Bergman
Layout: Lisa Schroeder

Publisher's Cataloging-In-Publication Data
Angel, Nikia.
    Easy crystal stitching : sophisticated jewelry / Nikia Angel.

    p. : col. ill. ; cm.

    ISBN: 978-0-87116-439-1

    1. Jewelry making--Handbooks, manuals, etc. 2. Beadwork--Handbooks, manuals, etc. I.
Title. II. Title: Crystal stitching

TT860 .A54 2012
745.594/2

Contents

Building Blocks

Projects

"As Bead ("Bede") is the ancient word for prayer, I bead with you in my heart. I hope it brings you happiness. I always feel so incredibly blessed that I'm able to spend my time creating and finding a way to share it with others. It truly makes my heart sing and my world go round."

Introduction

About a dozen years ago, I took a class from a local bead artist named Joanne Lucero to make a cute bracelet that she called the copycat bracelet. I made several. Then one day, I wasn't paying attention and my tension was all wonky—too loose in the middle and too tight on the edges. The strip of beadwork was curling in on itself. Since I don't like to un-bead, I decided to turn it into something else.

I wrapped the short piece around my finger and *boing*! A light went on. I would stitch the two ends together and make a sparkly wheel! At that time, an artist in Santa Fe was making beautiful little wheels from gold and semiprecious stones that she called story wheels—with all different stones and designs, they were beautiful. I decided I was going to make a bunch of my sparkly wheels in different colors and put them on a chain.

So, that's what I did. Word got around, and I taught them at a few informal occasions. I started selling the wheels. I started seeing others with bunches of sparkly wheels on chains! They became the beaded equivalent of potato chips: You can't make just one! There was a frenzy of people making the wheels, coming up with their own thread paths, and trading wheels. It is such a simple little design with so many possibilities, and it never fails to amaze me how changing a bead here and a bead there makes such a big difference.

In this book, I would like to give you a taste of some of the many designs I've made based on these little wheels (and there's more to come, I'm sure). I've also expanded the shapes to include triangles and squares, and added other elements (bails, bezels, spiral rope, and toggle clasps) to create the Building Blocks for the rest of the projects in the book. Choose your favorite shape and practice making a circle or two—or dive right in to the finished jewelry and refer back to the Building Blocks listed for each project as needed. The choice is yours!

I'm endlessly fascinated with the possibility of this incredibly simple little "thing"! I hope you will enjoy these projects and go off on your own path to create beautiful pieces that delight your heart and eyes.

Thank you, as always, for your support of my endeavors.

—Nikia

Materials and Tools

Let's Begin with Crystals

Crystal beads are made of the same materials that make up ordinary glass—sand, soda ash, and limestone—but have high lead oxide content. Most crystal beads have 10 to 35% lead oxide content. The lead-infused glass causes light to refract at a high level and gives crystals their trademark sparkle. Be sure that any crystals you use are free of abrasions, cuts, or flaws that may weaken your beading wire. The facets of the crystal should line up perfectly, and there should be no variation in shape or size from bead to bead. A variety of options are available for purchasing your crystals, but the best known are Swarovski, famous for their history, quality, and color, shape, and finish varieties.

Crystals can be found in many shapes, but I like to use bicones and rounds the most. They are available in a wide variety of finishes, like opaque or aurora borealis (AB), and colors, as well. I haven't listed the exact colors I used, so the sky's the limit! Look for similar shades, or create your own combinations.

Manufacturers also provide crystal or **glass pearls**, which are even and consistant—perfect for stitching. Choose from a wide variety of beautiful colors.

About Seed Beads

Seed beads come in packages, tubes, and hanks. A standard hank (a looped bundle of beads strung on thread) contains twelve 20-in. (51cm) strands. Tubes and packages are usually measured in grams and vary in size. Seed beads have been manufactured in many sizes ranging from the largest, 5º (also called E beads), which are about 5mm wide, to tiny size 20º or 22º, which aren't much larger than grains of sand. (The symbol º stands for aught or zero. The greater the number of aughts, the smaller the bead.) The most commonly available size in the widest range of colors is 11º, and I've used both 11º and 15º seed beads for the projects in this book.

Another type of seed bead is a **cylinder bead** (usually found in size 11º). Cylinders are very regular and have extremely large holes, which are useful for stitches requiring multiple thread passes. The beads fit together almost seamlessly, producing a smooth, fabric-like surface. You can substitute cylinders for seed beads in many of these pieces as well.

Seed beads are made with several types of glass: opaque, a solid-colored glass that light cannot pass through; translucent, a colored glass that light can pass through, but through which you can't see; and transparent, a clear or colored glass that you can see through. Transparent and translucent beads can be lined with colored glass or a colored, dyed, or painted lining. Silver- or gold-lined seed beads are lined with real silver or gold.

Glass seed bead finishes can be matte, semi-matte, satin, or shiny, and may also be treated with a variety of coatings. These include iris or aurora borealis (AB), which give multi-colored effects; pearlized (also called luster or ceylon); metallic (colored metal is fused to the glass surface); or galvanized (a rich but impermanent metallic coating).

TIP When working with seed beads, if you find your needle is getting stuck and you're having a hard time getting it through your beads, try switching to a smaller needle. This will potentially give you two or three more passes through that seed bead before the holes completely fill with thread.

Tools for Working with Seed Beads

My favorite tool is a pair of tweezers with a shovel on the end, or a **bead scoop shovel**. If you bend the shovel at a 45-degree angle, it is wonderful for picking up beads and putting them back where they belong. We pick up our beads and put them away right? Well, we're supposed to, anyway.

Another tool I use for beading is a pair of **gem-setter tweezers** (the ones with the extremely pointed ends). They are the best thing I have found for getting knots out of thread. If you wiggle the tips into the knot and then let go of the tweezers, they will spread open and hopefully open your knot.

Control your beading space with a lint-resistant **bead mat**. This mat will keep the tiny beads from rolling around your table.

If you like, dot your knots with E6000 or similar **glue**.

Tools

For the projects in this collection, I use **size 12 Sharps beading needles** and **Fireline 8 lb. test**. The thick Fireline is strong enough so the crystals won't cut through, and the size 12 needles are small enough to fit through tiny seed beads. (I can pass through 15º seed beads five to six times using a size 13 needle, so you can use that size as well.) One of the things Fireline is not good for is fringe. For fringe, I use **Nymo D**.

For some pieces, you'll use **chainnose pliers**, which have smooth, flat inner jaws, and tips that taper to a point. Use them for gripping and for opening and closing loops and jump rings. **Roundnose pliers** have smooth, tapered, conical jaws used to make loops. The closer to the tip you work, the smaller the loop will be. With **diagonal wire cutters**, use the front of the blades to make a pointed cut and the back of the blades to make a flat cut.

Other Materials

Clasps come in many sizes and shapes. You'll learn to make the toggle, consisting of a ring and a bar, out of crystals and seed beads in the Building Blocks section. If you choose a pre-made clasp, use a lobster claw, which opens when you pull a tiny lever; S-hook, which links two soldered jump rings or split rings; or hook-and-eye, consisting of a hook and a jump ring.

Earring findings come in a variety of metals and styles, including lever-back, post, hoop, and French hook. You will almost always want a loop (or loops) on earring findings so you can attach beads.

A **jump ring** is used to connect two components. It is a small wire circle or oval that is either soldered or comes with an opening.

A **headpin** looks like a long, thick, blunt sewing pin. It has a flat or decorative head on one end to keep the beads in place. Headpins come in different diameters, or gauges, and lengths ranging from 1–3 in. (2.5–7.6cm).

Chain is available in many finishes (sterling silver, gold-filled, base metal, plated metal) and styles (curb, figaro, long-and-short, rolo, cable). Often chain links can be opened in the same way loops and jump rings are opened. I've used finished chains with pre-attached clasps. If you prefer, cut a length of chain in the style you want and add whichever clasp you like.

Some projects require specialty materials, such as **bracelet blanks** and **Ultrasuede**.

Roundnose pliers

Beading needles

Chainnose pliers

Jewelry Techniques

Threading a Needle

To thread your needle, hold the piece of thread in your left hand with the end barely sticking out from between your fingers, move your needle toward that cut end, and, theoretically, the thread will go right through the eye of the needle. This may take some practice.

I have learned to thread my needle with the original cut end of the thread, not the end of the thread just cut. This will help prevent fraying and breaking, because when you thread the needle with the original cut end, the fibers in the thread are going in the way they were spun. If you thread the needle with the newly cut end, it goes against the fibers to fray and break the thread easier.

If you are having a hard time threading your needle, you can try turning your needle over. The eye of a needle is stamped when it is made, so on one side, the eye is concave and on the other, the eye is convex. This works better for me than the another alternative of needling the thread.

Knots and Thread

Half-hitch Knot

Pass the needle under the thread between two beads. A loop will form as you pull the thread through. Cross over the thread between the beads, sew through the loop, and pull gently to draw the knot into the beadwork.

Square Knot

Cross the left-hand end of the thread over the right, and bring it around and back up. Cross the end that is now on the right over the left, go through the loop, and pull both ends to tighten.

Ending/Adding Thread

For the projects in this book, ending and adding new threads are the same. To end your thread, you will simply weave in a zigzag pattern through your beadwork until your thread is secure. I prefer not to use knots, but feel free to tie a half-hitch knot here and there if you prefer.

To add a new thread, you'll do pretty much the same thing. Weave your thread in a zigzag fashion, using half-hitch knots if you prefer, until when you tug on the thread, it won't pull out. Then, pick up your beading where you left off. Because these pieces are made with components, each joining is a possible weak spot. Once you've completed making and joining the components, I recommend that you weave a single thread back through as many of them as you can. Fireline has a tendency to pull out of your beadwork, so I usually weave it through about twice as much as I would with Nymo.

Conditioning Thread

Use either beeswax (not candle wax or paraffin) or Thread Heaven to condition nylon thread (Nymo). Beeswax smooths the nylon fibers and adds tackiness that will stiffen your beadwork slightly. Thread Heaven adds a static charge that causes the thread to repel itself, so don't use it with doubled thread. Stretch the thread, then pull it through the conditioner, starting with the end that comes off the spool first.

Stop Bead

Use a stop bead to secure beads temporarily when you begin stitching. Choose a bead that is distinctly different from the beads in your project. String the stop bead about 6 in. (15cm) from the end of your thread, and go back through it in the same direction. If desired, go through it one more time for a little more security.

Half-hitch knot

Square knot

Stop bead

Tension

Tension refers to the general looseness or tightness of your beaded piece. When your tension is looser than you'd like it to be, you can stiffen your beadwork by sewing back through the seed beads and filling their holes with thread.

Remember: When you're learning something new, it's hard to maintain good tension and learn at the same time.

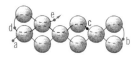

Peyote, even-count

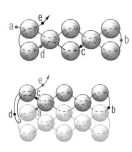

Peyote, odd-count

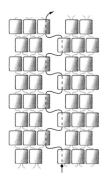

Zipping up or joining peyote

Stitching

For most projects, you will not be using a traditional stitching pattern—just follow the diagrams to complete the piece. However, a few projects are made with the basic flat peyote stitch, shown here.

Peyote, Even-Count

1 Pick up an even number of beads **(a–b)**. These beads will shift to form the first two rows (counted on the diagonal).

2 To begin row 3, pick up a bead, skip the last bead strung in the previous step, and sew through the next bead in the opposite direction **(b–c)**. For each stitch, pick up a bead, skip a bead in the previous row, and sew through the next bead, exiting the first bead strung **(c–d)**. The beads added in this row are higher than the previous rows and are referred to as "up-beads."

3 For each stitch in subsequent rows, pick up a bead, and sew through the next up-bead in the previous row **(d–e)**. To count peyote stitch rows, count the total number of beads along both straight edges.

Peyote, Odd-Count

Odd-count peyote is the same as even-count peyote, except for the turn on odd-numbered rows, where the last bead of the row can't be attached in the standard way because there is no up-bead to sew into. The odd-row turn can be convoluted, so I've simplified it here. Please note that the start of this simplified approach is a little different, because the first beads you pick up are the beads in rows 2 and 3. In the next step, you work row 1 and do a simplified turn. After

the turn, you'll work the rest of the piece, beginning with row 4.

1 Pick up an odd number of beads **(a–b)**. These beads will shift to form rows 2 and 3 in the next step. If you're working a pattern with more than one bead color, make sure you pick up the beads for the correct rows.

2 To begin the next row (row 1), pick up a bead, skip the last bead strung in the previous step, and sew through the next bead in the opposite direction **(b–c)**. Continue in this manner, exiting the second-to-last bead strung in the previous row **(c–d)**. For the final stitch in the row, pick up a bead, and sew through the first bead strung again **(d–e)**. The beads added in this row are higher than previous rows and are referred to as "up-beads."

3 To work row 4 and all other even-numbered rows, pick up one bead per stitch, exiting the end up-bead in the previous row **(a–b)**.

4 To work row 5 and all other odd-numbered rows, pick up one bead per stitch, exiting the end up-bead in the previous row **(b–c)**. Pick up a bead, and sew under the thread bridge between the edge beads below **(c–d)**. Sew back through the last bead added to begin the next row **(d–e)**.

Zipping Up or Joining Peyote

To join two sections of a flat peyote piece invisibly, match up the two pieces so the edge beads fit together. "Zip up" the pieces by zigzagging through the up-beads on both edges.

Plain loops

Wrapped loops

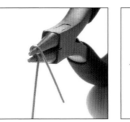 

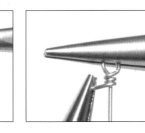

Wirework

Plain Loops

1 Using chainnose pliers, make a right-angle bend approximately ¼ in. (6mm) from the end of the wire.

2 Grip the tip of the wire in roundnose pliers. Press downward slightly, and rotate the wire into a loop.

3 Let go, then grip the loop at the same place on the pliers, and keep turning to close the loop.

4 The closer to the tip of the roundnose pliers that you work, the smaller the loop will be.

Wrapped Loops

1 Using chainnose pliers, make a right-angle bend approximately 1¼ in. (3.2cm) from the end of the wire.

2 Position the jaws of your roundnose pliers in the bend.

3 Curve the short end of the wire over the top jaw of the roundnose pliers.

4 Reposition the pliers so the lower jaw fits snugly in the loop. Curve the wire downward around the bottom jaw of the pliers. This is the first half of a wrapped loop.

5 To complete the wraps, grasp the top of the loop with chainnose pliers.

6 Wrap the wire around the stem two or three times. Trim the excess wire, and gently press the cut end close to the wraps with chainnose pliers.

Opening and Closing Loops or Jump Rings

1 Hold a loop or jump ring with two pairs of chainnose pliers or with chainnose and bentnose pliers.

2 To open the loop or jump ring, bring the tips of one pair of pliers toward you and push the tips of the other pair away.

3 Reverse the steps to close the loop or jump ring.

Opening and closing loops or jump rings

BUILDING BLOCKS

Begin with a simple, sparkly circle, which I also call a wheel. With this timeless shape as a foundation, you'll see hundreds of possibilities!

Materials
- **24** 4mm bicone crystals (or any 4mm bead)
- **1** gram 11º cylinder beads or seed beads
- beading needle and thread

Projects using a basic circle:

Circle

1 On 3 ft. (.9m) of thread, pick up an alternating pattern of a 4mm bicone crystal and an 11º cylinder bead until you have eight 4mms and eight cylinders, leaving a 6-in. (15cm) tail. Tie the beads into a ring with a square knot. Sew through the next 4mm and cylinder, and pull the thread to hide the knot **(figure 1)**.

2 Pick up five cylinders, skip the next 4mm, and sew through the following cylinder **(figure 2)**. Repeat to complete the round, and step up through the first three cylinders added in this step **(figure 3)**.

3 Pick up a cylinder, a 4mm, and a cylinder, skip five cylinders, and sew through the center cylinder in the next five-bead set. Repeat to complete the round **(figure 4)**. Retrace the thread path through the beads added in this step to reinforce, and exit a center cylinder between the 4mms along the outer edge **(figure 5)**.

4 Pick up five cylinders, and sew through the center cylinder between the next two 4mms along the outside edge **(figure 6)**. Repeat to complete the round, and step up through the first three cylinders added in this step **(figure 7)**. Don't worry about where the loops lie. They do not need to fit over the 4mms just added.

5 Pick up a 4mm, and sew through the center cylinder in the next five-bead set added in the previous round **(figure 8)**. Repeat to complete the round. Retrace the thread path to reinforce, and snug up the beads. End the threads.

Incorporate Pearls

To create a delicate, opulent look, use 4mm pearls in place of 4mm crystals as desired. You can even switch it up with other 4mm gemstone or glass beads—the combinations are endless!

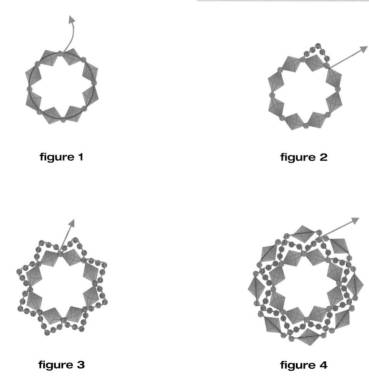

figure 1

figure 2

figure 3

figure 4

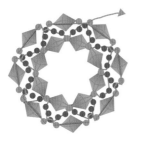

figure 5

figure 6

figure 7

figure 8

TRIANGLE

Projects using a basic triangle:

Bellagio Pendant and Earrings, *p. 56*

Once you've mastered the circle, try your hand at another basic shape: the triangle. With three straight edges, you can get a beautiful, geometric look.

Materials
- **21** 4mm bicone crystals (or any 4mm bead)
- **1** gram 11º cylinder beads or seed beads
- beading needle and thread

Triangle

1 On 3 ft. (.9m) of thread, pick up an alternating pattern of a 4mm bicone crystal and an 11º cylinder bead until you have six 4mms and six cylinders, leaving a 6-in. (15cm) tail. Tie the beads into a ring with a square knot. Sew through the next 4mm and cylinder, and pull the thread to hide the knot **(figure 1)**.

2 Pick up five cylinders, skip the next 4mm, and sew through the following cylinder. Repeat to complete the round, and step up through the first three cylinders added in this step **(figure 2)**.

3 Pick up a cylinder, a 4mm, a cylinder, a 4mm, and a cylinder, skip five cylinders, and sew through the center cylinder in the next five-bead set **(figure 3)**. Pick up a cylinder, a 4mm, and a cylinder, skip five cylinders, and sew through the center cylinder in the next five-bead set. Repeat these two stitches twice to complete the round. Retrace the thread path through the beads added in this step to reinforce, and exit the first 4mm at the next corner **(figure 4).**

figure 1

figure 2

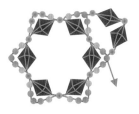

figure 3

figure 4

4 Pick up three cylinders, and sew through the next center 4mm. This cluster of beads on a corner is called a "picot." Sew through the beadwork to exit the first 4mm at the next corner. Repeat this stitch twice to complete the round, and sew through the beadwork to exit the first 4mm at the next corner **(figure 5)**.

5 Pick up five cylinders, and sew through the center cylinder in the next five-bead set **(figure 6)**. Repeat to complete the round **(figure 7)**. Retrace the thread path, and snug up the beads **(figure 8)**. End the threads.

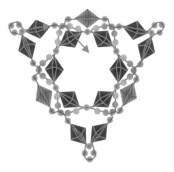

figure 5

figure 6

figure 7

figure 8

For even more options, add a square to your jewelry designs. This classic shape can also be turned on its side for a diamond silhouette.

Materials
- **28** 4mm bicone crystals (or any 4mm bead)
- **2** grams 11º cylinder beads or seed beads
- beading needle and thread

SQUARE

Projects using a basic square:

Square

1 On 3 ft. (.9m) of thread, pick up an alternating pattern of a 4mm bicone crystal and an 11º cylinder bead until you have eight 4mms and eight cylinders, leaving a 6-in. (15cm) tail. Tie the beads into a ring with a square knot. Sew through the next 4mm and cylinder, and pull the thread to hide the knot.

2 Pick up five cylinders, skip the next 4mm, and sew through the following cylinder. Repeat to complete the round, and step up through the first three cylinders added in this step.

3 Pick up a cylinder, a 4mm, a cylinder, a 4mm, and a cylinder, skip five cylinders, and sew through the center cylinder in the next five-bead set. Pick up a cylinder, a 4mm, and a cylinder, skip five cylinders, and sew through the center cylinder in the next five-bead set **(figure 1)**. Repeat these two stitches three times to complete the round. Retrace the thread path through the beads added in this step to reinforce, and exit the first 4mm at the next corner **(figure 2)**.

4 Pick up three cylinders, and sew through the next corner 4mm to make a picot. Sew through the beadwork to exit the first 4mm at the next corner. Repeat this step three times to complete the round **(figure 3)**.

5 Sew through the beadwork to exit the center cylinder in the next five-bead set added in step 2 (see **figure 3**). Pick up five cylinders, and sew through the center cylinder in the next five-bead set **(figure 4)**. Repeat to complete the round **(figure 5)**. Retrace the thread path, and snug up the beads. End the tail, if necessary, to keep it out of the way.

6 With the thread exiting a center cylinder in the five-bead set added in the previous round, pick up a 4mm, and sew through the center cylinder in the next five-bead set. Repeat to complete the round **(figure 6)**. Retrace the thread path, and snug up the beads. End the thread.

> ### Substitute Seed Beads
> For all of these shapes, you can subsitute seed beads for cylinder beads. Experiment to see the subtle difference, and choose whichever look you like—or whichever beads you have on hand!

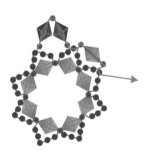

figure 1

figure 2

figure 3

figure 4

figure 5

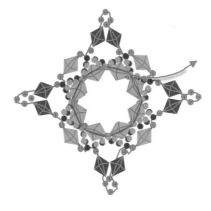

figure 6

BEZEL

Projects using a basic bezel:

Make a circle, triangle, or square to begin. The instructions for the bezel are the same, regardless of what shape you are making. For this example, I used a square.

Materials

- beads needed for circle, triangle, or square (see p. 11, 14, 17)
- 12mm crystal rivoli
- **1–2** grams 11º seed beads
- beading needle and thread

Bezel

1 Work as in steps 1–3 of basic circle (p. 11), basic triangle (p. 14), or basic square (p. 17) (**figure 1**, shown with square).

2 With the thread exiting the center 11⁰ cylinder bead in a three-bead set along the outer edge of the circle, pick up five cylinders, and sew through the center cylinder between the 4mm bicone crystals. Repeat to complete the round, and step up through the first three cylinders added in this step **(figure 2)**. Retrace the thread path through the beads and pull tight.

3 Insert the 12mm rivoli face down so the front of the rivoli rests on the 4mms in the initial ring created in step 1 of the basic circle, triangle, or square. With the thread exiting a center cylinder in a five-bead set added in the previous round, and working on the back of the rivoli, pick up three cylinders, and sew through the center cylinder in the next five-bead set **(figure 3)**. Pick up two cylinders, and sew through the center cylinder in the next five-bead set **(figure 4)**. Repeat these steps to complete the round. Step up through the first two cylinders added in this step **(figure 5)**.

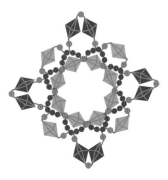

figure 1

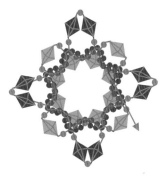

figure 2

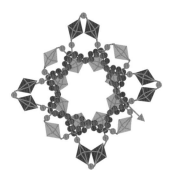

figure 3

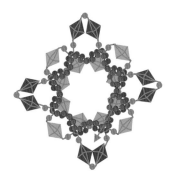

figure 4

4 Sew through the beadwork to exit a second 11º in a picot. Pick up three 11ºs, skip an 11º, and sew through the next six 11ºs **(figure 6)**. Continue adding picots until you are back where you started **(figure 7)**.

5 Sew through the beadwork to exit the second 11º in one of the picots. Pick up an 11º, and sew through the second 11º in the next picot **(figure 8)**. Repeat to complete the round.

6 Retrace the thread path and pull the thread tight.

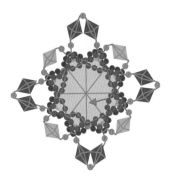

figure 5

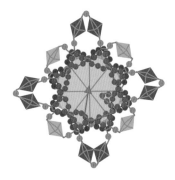

figure 6

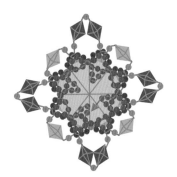

figure 7

figure 8

Hang a perfect pendant from this beautiful bail for a stylish, polished presentation.

Materials
- **9** 4mm crystals
- **1–2** grams 11º seed beads
- beading needle and thread

Front

1 On 12 in. (30cm) of thread, pick up an alternating pattern of a 4mm bicone crystal and an 11º seed bead three times, leaving a 6-in. (15cm) tail. Sew through all the beads again to form a ring. Tie a square knot.

2 Sew through the beads to exit an 11º **(figure 1)**. Pick up five 11ºs, skip the next 4mm, and sew through the next 11º. Repeat to complete the round, ending with your thread exiting the fourth 11º of a five-bead set **(figure 2)**.

3 Pick up an 11º, a 4mm, an 11º, a 4mm, and an 11º. Skip three 11ºs, and sew through the next three 11ºs. Repeat this stitch twice to complete the round. Sew through the beadwork to exit a 4mm **(figure 3)**.

4 Pick up three 11ºs, skip an 11º, and sew through the next two 11ºs and 4mm. Pick up three 11ºs, skip the next 11º, and sew through the following 4mm and next two 11ºs. Repeat to complete the round, and end the thread **(figure 4)**.

Back

1 Pick up six 11ºs, and sew back through all of the beads to form a ring. Tie a square knot, sew through the next two 11ºs, and pull to hide the knot.

2 Pick up three 11ºs, skip an 11º, and sew through the next 11º. Repeat this stitch two more times (**figure 5**, different bead colors used for clarity). Sew through the beadwork to exit the second 11º in the next three-bead set you just added.

3 Pick up five 11ºs, and sew through the second 11º in of the next three-bead set. Repeat to complete the round, and exit the second 11º in a five-bead set.

4 Pick up three 11ºs, skip the next 11º, and sew through the beadwork to exit the next five 11ºs. Repeat this stitch twice to complete the round.

5 Sew through the first 11º added in the previous round, pick up three 11ºs, skip the next 11º, and sew through the next seven 11ºs to exit the first 11º added in the next picot in the previous round. Repeat twice to complete the round (**figure 6**).

Connect the Bail

1 Exit the second 11º in an end picot of the back of the bail. Pick up an 11º, and sew through the second 11º of a three-bead picot on a corner of the front of the bail. Pick up an 11º, and sew back through the 11º your thread exited at the start of this step (**figure 7**).

2 Sew through the back of the bail to exit the center 11º in the next picot. Repeat this step on the other two corners of the back and front of the bail. Retrace the thread path through the last row on the bail, and reinforce the join several times. End the thread.

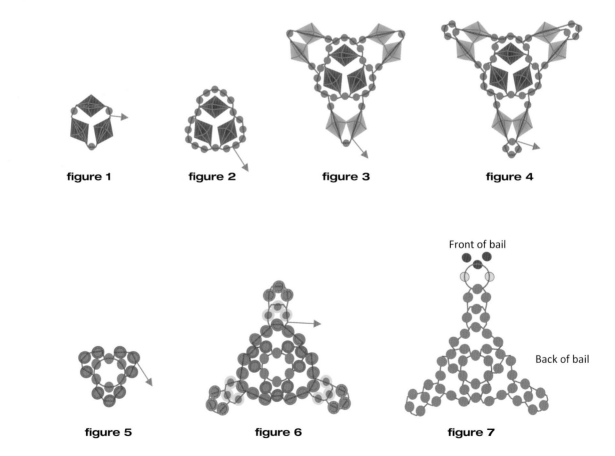

figure 1   figure 2   figure 3   figure 4

figure 5   figure 6   figure 7

Front of bail

Back of bail

24

Sometimes, the simplicity of a beautiful rope is the perfect way to present a stunning shape. Create this rope to showcase your circles, squares, and triangles with aplomb.

SPIRAL
ROPE

Projects using a spiral rope:

Graduated Wheels
Necklace, *p. 35*

Winter Skies Faux
Lariat, *p. 46*

Puerto de Luna
Necklace, *p. 62*

Materials
- **15–20** grams 11º seed beads
- beading needle and thread
- **30+** 4mm pearls or crystal bicones (optional)

Rope

1 Attach a stop bead to about 6–8 ft. (1.83–2.44m) of thread, and pick up seven 11º seed beads. Leave about a 6-in. (15cm) tail. Sew back through the first three 11ºs just picked up. Push the loop of beads to the left **(figure 1)**.

TIP If you only have one color of 11ºs, you might want to practice with two contrasting colors to make it easier to see the core. If you have two colors, pick up three core and four loop beads. Leave about a 12-in. (30cm) tail.

2 Pick up five 11ºs (one core bead and four loop beads) **(figure 2)**. Move the beads all the way down the thread, skip the first 11º of the core (the one the tail is exiting), and sew through the next three core beads and the first 11º you just picked up **(figure 3)**. Push the new loop to the left so it rests on the loop created in the previous step.

3 Pick up five 11ºs (one core and four loop beads), and sew through the next three core beads and first bead you just picked up. With every step, you will move up the core and the loops will spiral around the core in a diagonal fashion **(figures 4, 5)**. Continue to the desired length, ending and adding thread as needed.

TIP You may find it awkward to hang onto the first few beads as you stitch. I pinch the tail between my thumb and forefinger and lay the beadwork over my forefinger as I work.

| figure 1 | figure 2 | figure 3 | figure 4 | figure 5 |

Once you've created your masterpiece, finish it with a beautiful clasp. This simple toggle and bar makes perfect use of a shape you've already practiced.

TOGGLE CLASP

Projects using a toggle clasp:

Materials
- **26–30** 4mm bicone crystals (**26** for circle, **30** for square)
- **2** grams 11º cylinder beads or seed beads
- beading needle and thread

Toggle

Make a basic circle or square (p. 11 or 17, shown here with square), starting with eight 4mm bicone crystals and 11º cylinder beads. To join: With the thread exiting a cylinder between two 4mms, pick up six cylinders, and sew through one end of a bracelet or necklace. Pick up two cylinders, skip the last two cylinders picked up in the previous stitch, and sew through the next two cylinders. Pick up two cylinders, and sew through the same cylinder in the circle your thread exited **(figure 1)**. Retrace the thread path to secure. End the thread.

Bar

1 Pick up 12 cylinders or 11º seed beads. Skip the last cylinder, and sew back through the next-to-last cylinder bead. Pick up a cylinder, skip the next cylinder, and sew through the next cylinder. Continue in peyote stitch as shown in **figure 2** or in Stitching (p. 8) until you have 10 rows. (Count each row on the diagonal—for example, the illustration shows two rows.) Roll the strip into a tube shape, and zip it closed.

2 On one end of the tube, pick up a 4mm and a cylinder, skip the cylinder, and sew back through the 4mm and through the tube to the other end. Pick up a 4mm and a cylinder, skip the cylinder, and sew back through the 4mm and the tube. Retrace the thread path, and exit the center of the tube.

3 Attach the bar to the other end of the necklace or bracelet the same way you attached the toggle. If necessary, add more cylinders before sewing through the end of the bracelet to allow the bar room to slip through the toggle end of the clasp.

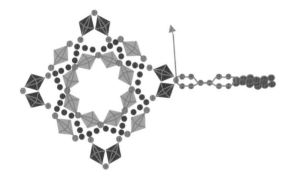

figure 1

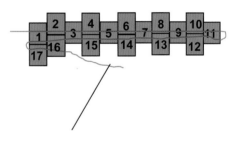

figure 2

PROJECTS

circle, p. 11

Wreath Earrings

When I think of circles, I immediately think about wreaths. Why not make a small, perfect pair for your ears?

Earrings

1 Make a basic circle (p. 11), starting with eight 4mm bicone crystals and eight 11º cylinder beads. Once the circle is complete, sew through the beadwork to exit the second cylinder of a three-bead set between the 4mms along the outside edge.

2 Pick up 10 green cylinders. Sew back through the cylinder your thread exited at the start of this step. Retrace the thread path to secure **(figure 1)**.

3 Pick up 10 red cylinders, and sew back through the same cylinder into the circle. Make another loop of 10 cylinders on the other side, and sew into the circle through the cylinder **(figure 2)**. End the thread.

4 Open the loop on an ear wire, and connect it to the top loop on the wreath.

5 Make another earring.

Materials

- **48** 4mm bicone crystals
- **2** grams 11º cylinder beads
- pair of ear wires
- beading needle and thread
- **2** pairs of flatnose or chainnose pliers

TIP
Create this piece in festive colors for Christmas (I chose emerald crystals and seed beads in red, green, and silver), or use elegant black crystals and cream pearls for year-round style.

figure 1

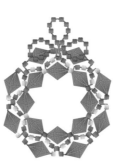

figure 2

Crystal Halo Pendant

If you can wear your heart on your sleeve, you can wear your halo around your neck! Let your inner angel shine with this beautiful, sparkling pendant.

circle,
p. 11

Materials

- **18** 4mm bicone crystals
- **36** 3mm bicone crystals
- **1–2** grams 11º cylinder beads
- **1–2** grams 15º seed beads
- 18 in. (46cm) small rope chain
- lobster claw clasp
- 3 in. (7.6cm) half-hard 22-gauge sterling silver wire
- beading needle and thread
- chainnose and roundnose pliers
- wire cutters

Pendant

This piece is simply a larger basic circle. Follow the directions exactly, or make an even bigger circle, if you like.

1 On 1 yd. (.9m) of thread, pick up a repeating pattern of a 3mm bicone crystal and an 11º cylinder bead until you have 18 3mms and 18 cylinders.

2 Sew through the beads again, and tie the beads into a ring with a square knot. Sew through the next 3mm and cylinder, and pull to hide the knot **(figure 1)**.

3 With your thread exiting one of the cylinders between the crystals, pick up two 15º seed beads, a cylinder, and two 15ºs, and sew through the next cylinder. Continue all the way around. End with the thread exiting the third bead of one of the five-bead sets (the cylinder) **(figure 2)**.

4 Pick up a 4mm bicone crystal, and sew through the center cylinder in the next five-bead set. Repeat to complete the round **(figure 3)**.

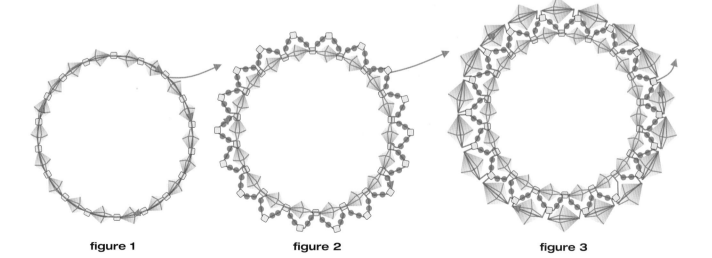

| figure 1 | figure 2 | figure 3 |

5 Retrace the thread path to maintain a tight tension. Reinforce each row multiple times to create as stiff a halo as possible. End with the thread exiting a cylinder in the last row.

6 Pick up two 15°s, a cylinder, and two 15°s, and sew through the next cylinder. Repeat to complete the round **(figure 4)**.

7 Sew through the beadwork to exit a cylinder in the center of a five-bead set from the previous step. Pick up a 3mm, and sew through the cylinder in the next five-bead set.

8 Repeat to complete the round. Retrace the thread path, and snug up the beads **(figure 5)**.

Add a Chain

1 You can thread the halo on a chain, or you can sew the chain to the wheel as shown on p. 32: Sew through the bottom link of half of the chain and a cylinder bead on the halo several times until secure.

2 If your chain has no clasp, you can finish off the chain by making two links and attaching them to the chain and a lobster clasp. To attach the clasp, make a wrapped loop on one end of the wire and attach it to the end link of chain.

3 String a 4mm on the wire. Attach the clasp with another wrapped loop.

4 On the other end link of the chain, make a figure-8 with the rest of your wire and the roundnose pliers: Wrap one end of the wire around the pliers at the fatter end, and then wrap the other end in the opposite direction, creating the figure-8. Attach to your chain.

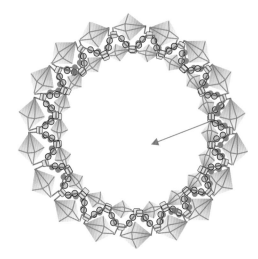

figure 4

figure 5

toggle clasp, p. 27

circle, p. 11

spiral rope, p. 25

Graduated Wheels Necklace

This necklace is composed of a series of sparkly circles made from pearls and crystals in graduated sizes threaded onto a spiral rope. Start by making the largest circle in the center.

Materials

- **62** 4mm bicone crystals
- **120** 4mm crystal or freshwater pearls
- **20** grams 11º seed beads in **1** or **2** colors
- **5** grams 11º cylinder beads to match seed beads
- beading needle and thread
- dowel or pencil (optional)

Create the Circles

Make a total of eight basic circles (p. 11), but follow the steps below to change the size and types of beads.

1 Make two circles with nine sets of 11º cylinder beads and 4mm pearls in step 1, 4mm bicone crystals in step 3, and pearls in step 4.

2 Make two circles with eight sets of cylinders and pearls in step 1, crystals in step 3, and pearls in step 4.

3 Make two circles with seven sets of cylinders and pearls in step 1, crystals in step 3, and pearls in step 4.

4 Make two circles with six sets of cylinders and pearls in step 1, crystals in step 3, and pearls in step 4.

Stitch the Rope

1 On a comfortable length of thread, leaving an 8-in. (20cm) tail, thread a needle and pick up seven 11º seed beads. Skip the last four beads, and sew back up through the first three 11ºs **(figure 1)**.

TIP If you are using one color of seed beads, you might want to practice for a little bit with two contrasting colors to make it easier to see the core. If you have two colors, you will pick up four core beads and three loop beads.

2 Pick up four or five 11ºs (one core and three or four loop beads if you have two colors) **(figure 2)**.

3 Move the beads all the way down the thread, skip the first bead of the core (the one the tail is coming out of), and sew through the next three or four core beads and one core bead just added **(figure 3)**.

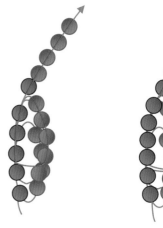

figure 1   figure 2   figure 3   figure 4   figure 5

4 Pick up four or five more 11⁰s (one core and three or four loop beads, if you have two colors), and sew through the next three or four core beads and the first bead you just added **(figure 4)**. With every step, you will move up the core. The loops will spiral around the core in a diagonal fashion **(figure 5)**.

5 Continue until the rope is about 10 in. (25cm) long (if you are making an 18-in./46cm rope), or a little more than half of the finished length, adding and ending thread as needed.

String the Circles

For the smaller circles, if you twist the circle as you put it on the rope, it will move up the rope easily.

1 String a six-bead circle and a seven-bead circle. Then string the eight-bead circle and finally one of the nine-bead circles, making sure they all fit. If they do, take them off until you bead the rope a little longer.

2 If the circles are too tight, use a thin dowel or a pencil to enlarge the hole. Wiggle the center to loosen it up so that it fits over the rope snugly.

3 Continue to stitch the rope a few more inches, and then slide on all the circles in this order: a six, a seven, an eight, a nine, an eight, a seven, and a six.

4 With about ½ in. (1.3cm) of the rope sticking out of the six-bead circle, continue to work the spiral rope until it is about 1 in. (2.5cm) shorter than the desired finished length.

5 Reinforce the core and loop beads at the end of the rope. When they are secure, end the thread.

Make the Toggle

Attach the remaining circle to the reinforced end of the spiral rope. This serves as half of the toggle clasp.

1 With your thread exiting the end of the rope, pick up three 11⁰s and sew through one of the cylinder beads in the circle next to a crystal.

2 Sew through the next two cylinders in the circle, pick up three cylinders, and sew back down through the rope. Retrace the thread path through the join **(figure 6)**.

3 Weave your thread in a zigzag fashion through a loop, the core, a loop, etc. until it is secure.

4 Thread a needle on the tail on the other end of the rope, and reinforce the end of the rope and the first two loops until you can't get the needle through anymore. Sew up through the core and loop beads in a zigzag fashion until they are secure, and end the thread.

5 Make a toggle bar (p. 27), and attach it to the other end of the spiral rope.

TIP Be sure to keep taut tension throughout—the stiffer your circles are, the better.

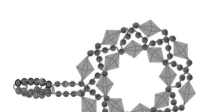

figure 6

Bling Ring

Don't let the sparkle stop at your neck or wrist—add glitter to your fingers with this glamorous, eye-catching ring.

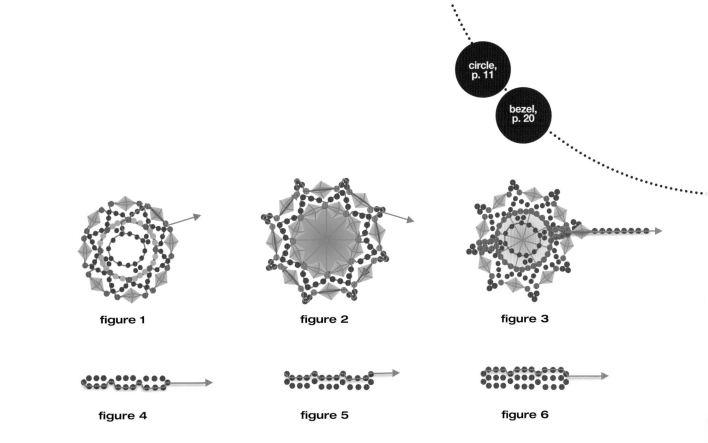

circle, p. 11

bezel, p. 20

figure 1

figure 2

figure 3

figure 4

figure 5

figure 6

Materials
- 12mm crystal rivoli
- **18** 4mm bicone crystals
- **2** grams 11º cylinder beads or seed beads
- beading needle and thread
- glue (optional)

Ring

1 Work a basic circle, steps 1–3 (p. 12), using eight 4mm bicone crystals and 11º cylinder beads.

2 Make a bezel (p. 20), and exit the first cylinder next to a 4mm along the outer edge (**figure 1**, back).

3 Pick up three cylinders, skip a cylinder, and sew through a cylinder and the next 4mm. Add picots in this manner all the way around the circle (**figure 2**, front).

4 Sew through the beadwork to exit the third bead of one of the loops on the last row you added at the back of your work (the one that is all cylinders) (**figure 3**, back).

5 Pick up three cylinders and a 4mm. Then pick up enough cylinders to fit your finger snugly.

6 Pick up a 4mm and three cylinders, and sew through the third bead in the loop directly across from where you started.

7 Sew through the beadwork to exit the cylinder that is the third bead in the next loop. Pick up three cylinders, and sew through the 4mm again.

8 Count the number of beads on the finger ring portion between the crystals. If the number is divisible by four, pick up three cylinders, skip three cylinders, and sew through the next cylinder. Repeat this stitch until you reach the next 4mm (**figure 4**).

If the number is divisible by three, pick up two cylinders, skip two cylinders, and sew through the next cylinder. Repeat until you reach the next 4mm.

9 Sew through the 4mm, and pick up three cylinders.

10 Sew through the corresponding cylinder in the circle. Sew through the beadwork to exit the first four beads added in step 5.

11 Sew through the next two or three cylinders, depending on how many you went through in step 8 (**figure 5**). Pick up a cylinder, and sew through the next two (or three) cylinders. Repeat this stitch to complete the round (**figure 6**).

12 Retrace the thread path to secure, and end the thread. Knot and glue, if desired.

TIP
Try using two different crystal shades for an even more colorful creation.

Que Linda Necklace

Glam up a little black dress—or a plain T-shirt
and jeans—with this showstopper. This opulent,
reversible necklace is sure to turn heads!

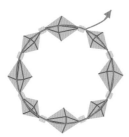

figure 1

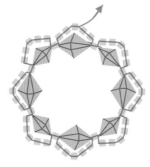

figure 2

circle,
p. 11

Materials

- **24** 6mm bicone crystals
- **134–142** 4mm crystal pearls
- **215–229** 4mm bicone crystals
- **9** 3mm bicone crystals
- **10** grams 11º cylinder beads
- sterling silver toggle clasp
- **2** beading needles and thread
- chainnose pliers (optional)
- glue (optional)

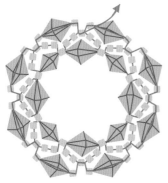

figure 3

figure 4

Make the Lower Center Circle

1 On 3 ft. (.9m) of conditioned thread, pick up a repeating pattern of a 6mm bicone crystal, an 11º cylinder, a 4mm bicone crystal, and a cylinder four times, leaving a 6-in. (15cm) tail. Tie the beads into a ring with a square knot. Sew through all the beads again to reinforce, and exit a cylinder **(figure 1)**.

2 Pick up five cylinders, skip the next crystal, and sew through the following cylinder. Pick up five cylinders, skip a crystal, and sew through the following cylinder. Repeat to complete the round, and step up through the first three cylinders added in this round **(figure 2)**.

3 Pick up a cylinder, a 6mm crystal, and a cylinder. Sew through the third cylinder in the next five-bead set in the previous round. Repeat to complete the round, and retrace the thread path through all the beads in this round.

4 End with your thread exiting the second cylinder in the set of three between the crystals along the outer edge of the ring **(figure 3)**.

5 Pick up five cylinders, skip a cylinder, a crystal, and a cylinder, and sew through the next cylinder. Repeat to complete the round, and step up through the third cylinder in the next loop of five **(figure 4)**.

6 Pick up a 6mm crystal, and sew through the third cylinder in the next loop of five. Pick up a 4mm crystal, and sew through the third cylinder in the next loop of five. Repeat these two stitches to complete the round. Retrace the thread path through all the beads added in this round, keeping a tight tension. Sew through the beadwork to exit a cylinder next to a 6mm crystal along the outer edge **(figure 5)**.

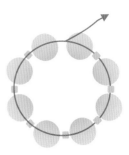

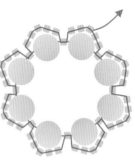

figure 5

figure 6

figure 7

figure 8

7 Pick up five cylinders, a 3mm bicone crystal, a 4mm crystal, a 6mm crystal, and a cylinder. Skip the last cylinder, and sew back through the crystals and the next cylinder. Pick up four cylinders, skip the 6mm crystal, and sew through the cylinder on the other side. End the threads **(figure 6)**.

Make a Side Circle

Stitch a sparkly circle to join to the "Lower Center Circle." (This circle and the remaining circles have pearls on the inner ring on the front and crystals on the back.)

1 On 2 ft. (61cm) of thread, leaving a 3-in. (7.6cm) tail, pick up a repeating pattern of a cylinder and a pearl until you have eight (or nine) pearls and eight (or nine) cylinders. Tie the beads into a ring with a square knot. Retrace the thread path, and exit a cylinder **(figure 7)**.

2 Pick up five cylinders, skip the next pearl, and sew through the following cylinder. Repeat to complete the round, and step up

through the first three cylinders added in this round **(figure 8)**.

3 Pick up a cylinder, a 4mm crystal, and a cylinder. Sew through the second cylinder in the next set of five. Repeat to complete the round, stopping just before adding the last 4mm crystal.

Complete the Three-Circle Centerpiece

1 With the thread exiting a cylinder in the side circle, sew through a 6mm along the outer edge of the lower center circle. Pick up a cylinder, and and sew through the third cylinder in the next loop of five in the side circle **(figure 9)**. Retrace the thread path through all the beads in this round, exiting the third cylinder in a loop of five **(figure 10)**.

2 Next, add a ring of crystals that will sit behind the ring of pearls: Pick up a 4mm crystal, and sew through the third cylinder bead of the next loop of five. Repeat this stitch to complete the round, and then retrace the thread path, keeping

a tight tension. Weave the thread back through all beads on this ring and pull taut **(figure 11**, back).

3 Repeat "Make a Side Circle." Repeat steps 1 and 2 to connect it to the other side of the centerpiece **(figure 12)**.

4 Next, add 6mm crystals to the two side circles above the lower center circle in the centerpiece: Sew through the beadwork and exit a side cylinder as shown in **figure 13**. Pick up a cylinder, a 6mm crystal, and a cylinder, and sew into the corresponding bead directly across on the other side circle.

5 Sew through the beadwork and exit a side cylinder further up on the side circle as shown in **figure 13**. Pick up a cylinder, a 6mm crystal, a cylinder, a 6mm crystal, and a cylinder, and sew through the corresponding bead directly across on the other side circle **(figure 13**, back).

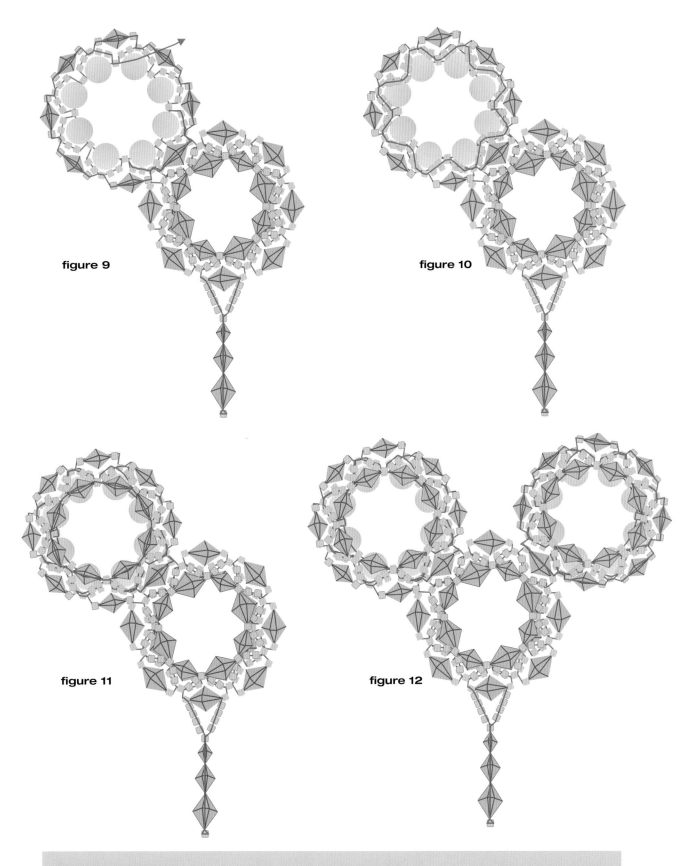

figure 9

figure 10

figure 11

figure 12

Reversible Necklace
Use pearls for demure glamour, as in the instructions, or choose crystals only for extra sparkle. I used 4mm
pearls for one side of the rings on each circle except the first one, so the necklace is reversible. Flaunt
whichever side suits your mood!

Build the Sides

1 Make more circles for each side, connecting them to the previous circles as in "Complete the Three-Circle Centerpiece," steps 1 and 2. To make the piece as in the illustrations, make three eight-bead circles, a seven-bead circle, and a six-bead circle. To make the piece as in the photo, make a nine-bead circle, two eight-bead circles, and two seven-bead circles.

2 If desired, make an eight-bead circle and attach it to the first and second circles (**figure 14**, back). For this circle, skip two 4mm crystals, attaching the circle in two places as in "Complete the Three-Circle Centerpiece," steps 1 and 2.

3 Attach a swag from one wheel to another (see photo on p. 40): A swag is composed of three cylinders, a 3mm crystal, three cylinders, a 4mm pearl, three cylinders, a 4mm crystal, three cylinders, a 4mm pearl, three cylinders, a 6mm crystal, three cylinders, a 4mm pearl, three cylinders, a 4mm crystal, three cylinders, a 4mm pearl, three cylinders, a 3mm crystal, and three cylinders. Attach to the appropriate crystal, and then sew through the beadwork to the next crystal where you want the swag. Repeat and attach at the appropriate crystal.

Neck Straps

1 Thread a needle on each end of 1 yd. (.9m) of thread, and center 10 cylinders and half the clasp on the thread. With the right-hand needle, sew back through all the cylinders and the clasp to form a ring. Pull the thread tight.

2 With the right-hand needle, pick up five cylinders and a 4mm pearl. With the left-hand needle, pick up five cylinders, and

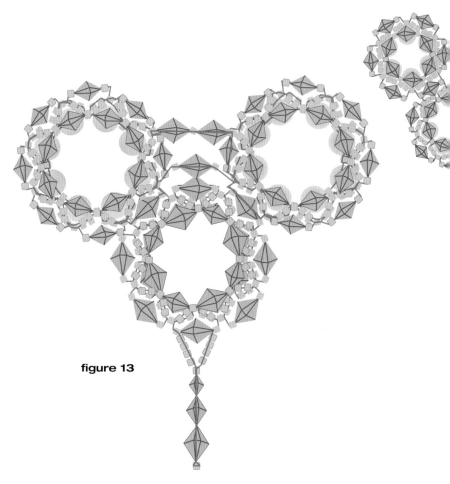

figure 13

cross through the pearl picked up by the other needle.

3 With the left-hand needle, pick up five cylinders and a 3mm crystal. With the right-hand needle, pick up five cylinders, and cross through the 3mm crystal picked up on the other needle.

4 Repeat steps 2 and 3 until you have reached the desired length. Then, pick up five cylinders on each needle and cross through a 4mm crystal along the outer edge of an end circle.

5 With each needle, sew back through the last two cylinders added in the previous step. Pick up three cylinders, skip a cylinder, and sew through the next two cylinders in the neck strap. Repeat to the end of the necklace **(figure 15)**.

6 Repeat on the other end of the necklace. Use a pair of chainnose pliers, if necessary, to help pull the needle through the crystal.

7 When you get picots on either side of the loops, sew through the beadwork until secure. Knot and glue, if desired, and end the thread.

figure 14

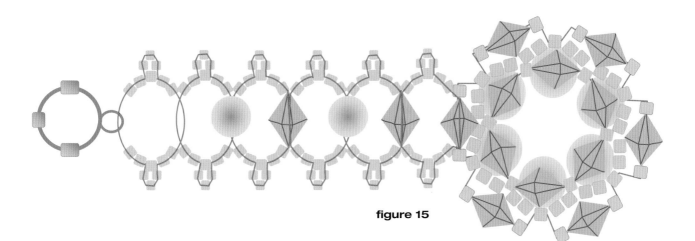

figure 15

Winter Skies
Faux Lariat

Create this dazzling rope to adorn your neck with flair.

Glittering dangles add a touch of elegance, while a

single, beautiful circle takes center stage.

Make Half with Circle

1 Make a basic circle (p. 11), starting with nine sets of 4mm bicone crystals and 11º cylinder beads. Set aside.

2 Make a loop on one end of the rope that will fit around the bead or button you plan to use for the other end: Pick up 15–20 color B 11º seed beads, or as many as needed to fit around the bead or button, and tie the beads into a loop. Pick up four B 11ºs and three A 11º seed beads to start the spiral rope, and continue as instructed to make a basic spiral rope (p. 25).

3 Make the spiral rope 6–6½ in. (15–16.5cm) long. Continue to work the spiral rope, but from this point on, for every fourth loop, pick up an A 11º, a 4mm, and an A 11º, and sew through the core beads. Then sew through three regular loops and a crystal loop. Continue until the piece is 9 in. (23cm) long.

4 Stitch the circle to the end of the spiral rope, exiting an end core bead. Pick up three B 11ºs, and sew through one of the crystals on the outer ring of the circle. Pick up three B 11ºs, and sew back down through the core. Weave the thread through the loops and core until it is secure, and end the thread. Glue, if desired.

Make Half with Fringe

1 Begin a second spiral rope. After you have made about 1 in. (2.5cm) of the spiral rope, sew back through the core and add the bead or button you want to use as a clasp to the end. (I used a druk and a puffy rondelle bead.)

2 If using a bead, pick up the bead and an 11º, skip the 11º, and sew back down through the bead(s) and into the core. Sew through the beadwork to exit the end bead in the core, and continue your spiral rope.

3 When the rope is 6½ in. (16.5cm) long, thread the rope through the circle on the first section of spiral rope, and start adding 4mm crystals to this section as in step 3 of "Make Half with Circle." Continue the spiral rope until it is 11½ in. (29.2cm) long.

4 To make fringe, which will keep the circle from sliding, on one of the spiral rope, pick up 3 in. (7.6cm) of assorted 11ºs and crystals. Do a three-bead turn around: Skip three beads, sew back into the fourth bead, and then sew back through all the beads added in this step. This completes one basic fringe.

5 If desired, add picots at any point along the fringe by exiting a bead, picking up three 11ºs, skipping a bead, and sewing back up through several more beads.

TIP If you have trouble getting your needle through the core, switch to a size 13 needle. Also, you can use chainnose pliers to gently pull your needle through a tight bead. Wiggle the needle slightly as you pull.

circle, p. 11

spiral rope, p. 25

Materials
- 10–12mm button or large bead to use as clasp
- **80–100** 4mm bicone crystals
- 11º seed beads
  - **6** grams color A
  - **15** grams color B
- **1** gram 11º cylinder beads
- beading needle and thread
- glue (optional)

6 When you reach the top of the fringe, sew back up through a few core beads, and sew back down to exit the beadwork. Begin another fringe.

7 Continue in this manner until your tassel is as full as you want. Weave the thread through the loops and core until it is secure, and end the thread. Glue, if desired.

TIP Try using two different crystal colors for an even more colorful creation.

Rivoli Revelry Bracelet

Get out your sunglasses!

This extra-sparkly bracelet

is a stunner!

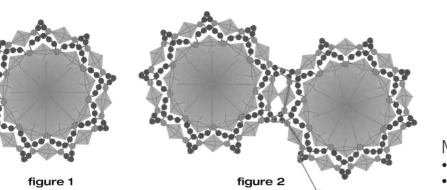

figure 1

figure 2

Materials

bezel, p. 20

toggle clasp, p. 27

- **7** 14mm crystal rivolis
- **155** 4mm bicone crystals
- **10** grams 11º cylinder beads
- beading needle and thread

figure 3

Bracelet

Make the first circle, and then connect circles to the previous circle after adding the rivoli.

1 Follow the instructions for a basic bezel (p. 20), using nine crystals and nine cylinders. Work picots on the outer edge as step 3 of the Bling Ring (p. 38). Reinforce several times, and end the threads **(figure 1)**.

2 Make a second bezeled rivoli, but before you work the picots, join it to the previous bezeled rivolis: With your thread exiting an 11º next to a crystal along the outer edge, pick up an 11º, and sew through the next center 11º in a picot on the first bezeled rivoli. Pick up an 11º, and sew through the cylinder next to a crystal on the circle where you are adding/joining the picots.

3 Sew through the next crystal and 11º. Pick up an 11º, and sew through the center 11º in the next picot in the first bezeled rivoli. Pick up an 11º, and sew through the next 11º, crystal, and 11º in the unfinished bezeled rivoli. Pick up an 11º **(figure 2, shows completed bezel)**.

4 Continue to work picots as in step 1 to complete the round (see **figure 2**).

5 Repeat steps 2–4 until you have seven bezeled rivolis (or until the bracelet is 1 in./2.5cm shorter than the desired length).

TIP Pay attention to what picots you attach the circles to as you go, because that will change the shape of your bracelet **(figure 3)**.

6 Once you have joined all of the bezeled rivolis, make a toggle clasp (p. 27) to complete the bracelet. (For this toggle bar, I added a three-bead picot on each end.) Attach the toggle bar to an end bezeled rivoli **(figure 4)**. Attach the circle half of the toggle clasp to the other end of the bracelet by sewing through the appropriate "peak" bead on one of the picots **(figure 5)**.

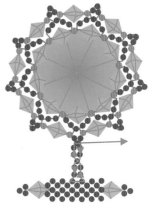

figure 4

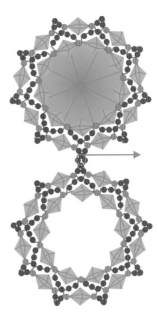

figure 5

Arabesque Bracelet

Make a more delicate version of the square with this

modified bracelet. Although the strap is thinner, bright color

combinations pack a real visual punch.

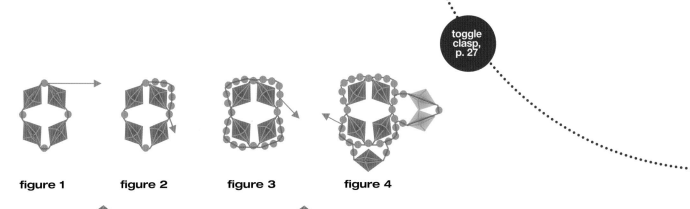

figure 1   **figure 2**   **figure 3**   **figure 4**

toggle clasp, p. 27

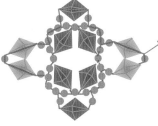

figure 5

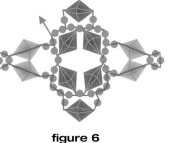

figure 6

Materials
- 4mm bicone crystals
  - **28–34** color A
  - **26–28** color B
- **3–4** grams 11º seed beads
- beading needle and thread

Bracelet

1 Pick up an alternating pattern of an 11º seed bead and a color A 4mm bicone crystal four times. Tie the beads into a ring with a square knot, and sew through the beads in the ring again **(figure 1)**.

2 Sew through the beadwork to exit an 11º. Pick up five 11ºs, skip the next A, and sew through the next 11º **(figure 2)**. Repeat to complete the round. Step up through the first four beads added in this round **(figure 3)**.

3 Pick up an 11º, a color B 4mm bicone crystal, an 11º, a B, and an 11º. Skip the next three 11ºs, and sew through the following three 11ºs.

4 Pick up an 11º, an A, and an 11º, skip the next three 11ºs, and sew through the next three 11ºs **(figure 4)**. Pick up an 11º, a B, an 11º, a B, and an 11º. Skip the next three 11ºs, and sew through the following three 11ºs. Pick up an 11º, an A, and an 11º. Skip the next three 11ºs, and sew through the next three 11ºs. Step up through the first 11º and B added at the start of this round **(figure 5)**. Pick up three 11ºs, skip the next 11º in the previous round,

and sew through the following B. Sew through the beadwork to exit the next B, and repeat this stitch **(figure 6)**. End the thread, and set the component aside.

5 Make a second component, but when you reach the point of adding the picots between the Bs in step 4, join to the first component: Exiting the first B, pick up an 11º, and sew through the center 11º in the picot of the first component. Pick up an 11º, and sew through the next B in the second component.

6 Continue to make and join subsequent components until your bracelet is 1 in. (2.5cm) shorter than the desired length.

Toggle Ring

1 Make sure you have at least 3 ft. (.9m) of thread on your needle. With the thread exiting one end of the bracelet, pick up three 11ºs, an A, three 11ºs, an A, three 11ºs, an A, and three 11ºs, and sew back through the first bead.

2 Sew through the first three 11ºs, A, and 11º added in the previous round. Pick up three 11ºs,

skip an 11º in the previous round, and sew through the next 11º, A, and 11º. Repeat this step to complete the round.

3 Retrace the thread path through the last round to reinforce, and sew through to the other end of the bracelet, reinforcing all the joins. End the thread.

Toggle Bar

1 Make a toggle bar (p. 27). Exit the middle of the bar, pick up five 11ºs, and sew through the top bead of a picot on the end of the bracelet opposite the toggle ring.

2 Pick up two 11ºs, and sew through the center 11º in the five-bead set added in the previous step. Pick up two 11ºs, and sew back through the peyote tube. Retrace the thread path, and end the threads.

TIP If you need a longer bracelet, make the portion of the necklace from the toggle bar to the bracelet slightly longer.

Showstopper Ring

Perfect for a cocktail party or dressy event, this ring is easy and eye-catching. You might want to make several in different colors.

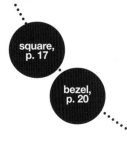

Materials

- 14mm crystal rivoli
- **36** 4mm bicone crystals in **1** or **2** colors
- **2** grams 11º cylinder beads
- beading needle and thread
- glue (optional)

Make and Embellish the Bezel

1 Follow steps 1–3 of the basic square (p. 17), using different colors of 4mm bicone crystals as desired. Insert the 14mm rivoli, and create a basic bezel (p. 20).

2 Sew through the beadwork to exit a 4mm on the inside edge, next to the rivoli. You will be adding 4mms to "stand up" on the surface of the ring. Pick up a 4mm and an 11º cylinder bead **(figure 1)**; skipping the cylinder, sew back through the 4mm next to the rivoli and the next 4mm in the original ring. Repeat to complete the round. If you are having a hard time getting through the beads, switch to a size 13 needle. Retrace the thread path to reinforce.

3 Sew through the beadwork to exit a first 11º in a set of three 11ºs between the 4mms along the outside edge of the initial square. Pick up a 4mm and a cylinder, skip the last cylinder, and sew back down through the 4mm. Skip the center cylinder in the three-bead set, and sew through the next cylinder, 4mm, and cylinder. Repeat to complete the round, and retrace the thread path to reinforce.

Finish the Ring

1 Sew through the beadwork to the back of the ring, exiting a cylinder next to a 4mm on the corner if you want a diamond-shaped ring, or in the middle if you want a square **(figure 2)**.

2 Pick up enough beads to fit around your finger. Make the band a couple of beads larger than you need, as it will tighten up. Sew through the corresponding cylinder on the other side of the bezel, the adjacent 4mm, and the next cylinder. Pick up three cylinders, skip the last three cylinders picked up, and sew through the next two cylinders.

3 Work in two-drop peyote: Work as in regular peyote, but pick up or skip two beads instead of one in each step. Sew back across the ring portion. Work another row, and end the thread **(figure 3)**.

4 Weave your thread until it is secure, and cut. Knot and glue, if desired.

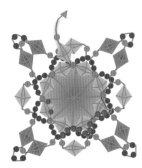

figure 1

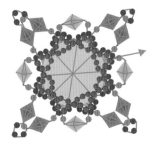

figure 2

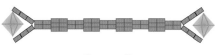

figure 3

Venezia
Pendant

This pendant and bail are deceptively simple and quick to make.

Follow the instructions for the pendant on the left, or use pearls

and embellish the bail as desired for the alternate on the right.

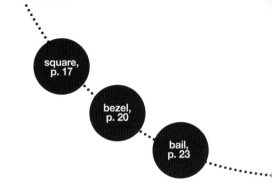

square, p. 17

bezel, p. 20

bail, p. 23

Materials
- 12mm crystal rivoli
- 4mm bicone crystals
  - **22** color A
  - **18** color B
- **2–3** grams 15º seed beads
- 18 in. (46cm) gold rope chain with clasp
- beading needle and thread

Pendant

1 Make a basic square with a bezeled rivoli (p. 20). Use 15º seed beads and color A and color B 4mm bicone crystals as shown.

2 Make a component using 15ºs, As, and Bs as shown in the Arabesque Bracelet (p. 50), "Bracelet" steps 1–4. if desired, reinforce by sewing bands of 15ºs criss-crossing on the back of the component. Add a picot at one end: With the thread exiting the middle 15º in the three-bead set, pick up an A and three or four 15ºs, and sew back through the first 15º picked up and the A.

3 Join the bezel and component together by connecting the 15ºs on the edges. Reinforce **(figure 1)**.

4 Make a basic bail (p. 23).

5 To complete the bail and join the pieces, sew through the beadwork to exit a B on a corner of the bail. Pick up a 15º, and sew through the second 15º in one of the picots on the square portion of the pendant.

6 Pick up a 15º, and sew through the 11º and B in the bail. Retrace the thread path through the last row to reinforce **(figure 2)**. End the threads.

7 String the chain through the bail.

figure 1

figure 2

Bellagio Pendant and Earrings

Dangle a drop from a chain with this flashy yet understated pair. Choose a long or short version of the earring to complement your finished necklace.

triangle, p. 14

bezel, p. 20

Materials

Necklace
- 12mm crystal rivoli
- 4mm bicone crystals
  - **16** color A
  - **10** color B
- **2** grams 11º seed beads
- 18 in. (46cm) rope chain with attached clasp
- **2** 6mm oval jump rings
- wire cutters

Earrings
- 4mm bicone crystals
  - **14** color A
  - **8** color B
- **2** grams 11º seed beads
- pair of earring wires

Both
- beading needle and thread
- **2** pairs of chainnose or flatnose pliers

Necklace

1 Make a basic triangle (p. 14) with color A and B 4mm bicone crystals and 11º seed beads. Use the photo as a guide for bead placement.

2 Insert the 12mm rivoli, and complete the bezel (p. 20). Use 11ºs for the back of the bezel. Retrace the thread path several times to secure.

3 With your thread exiting a 4mm on a point of the triangle, pick up three 11ºs, and sew through the next 4mm on the same corner of the triangle. Sew through the beadwork to exit a 4mm at the next corner. Repeat this stitch to complete the round, and end the threads **(figure 1)**.

figure 1

figure 2

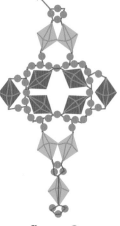

figure 3

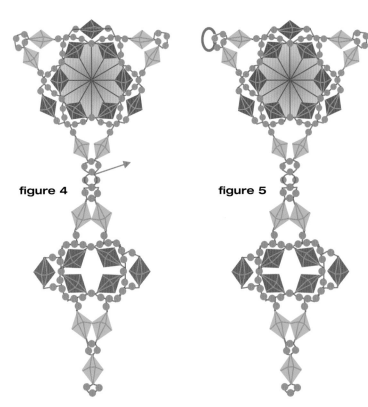

figure 4

figure 5

7 To add the necklace: Locate the center of the chain, and cut it into two pieces.

8 Open a 6mm oval jump ring, and string the picot on the top corner of the pendant and the bottom link of one half of the chain **(figure 5)**. Close the jump ring tightly. Repeat on the other side.

Earrings

1 Follow "Necklace" steps 4 and 5 to make a component. At the top of the component, pick up six to eight 11º seed beads, and sew back through the first 11º to make a loop. Retrace the thread paths to reinforce. Attach the loop to an ear wire.

2 Make a second earring.

3 To make a longer earring: Pick up 20–25 11ºs, sew through the loop of the earring wire, skip five 11ºs, and sew back into the next 11º. Continue stitching back to the component, picking up an 11º and skipping every other 11º as you go.

4 Make sure you have at least 24 in. (61cm) of thread on the needle. Make a component using 11ºs, As, and Bs as shown in the Arabesque Bracelet (p. 50), "Bracelet" steps 1–4, only adding a picot on one end **(figure 2)**.

5 With the thread exiting the 11º on the end without a picot, pick up an A and three 11ºs, and sew back through the A. Pick up one or two 11ºs (one for the pendant, two for the earrings as shown), and sew through the A and 11ºs as shown in **figure 3**.

6 Sew through the beadwork to exit a center 11º in the picot at the other end of the component. Join the two pieces together: Pick up an 11º, and sew through the center 11º in the next picot in the triangle. Pick up an 11º, and sew through the other side of the 11º your thread exited at the start of this step **(figure 4)**. Retrace the thread path to secure the join, and end the threads.

square,
p. 17

bezel,
p. 20

toggle
clasp,
p. 27

Materials

- **3** 12mm crystal rivolis
- **62** 4mm Czech fire-polished beads
- **58** 4mm glass pearls
- **5** grams 11º cylinder beads
- beading needle and thread

Bits 'n Pieces Bracelet

This bracelet is a combination of a lot of odds and ends. Enjoy the flash and flare of beautiful pearls and crystals on your wrist!

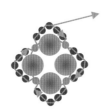

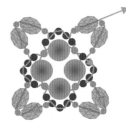

figure 1

figure 2

figure 3

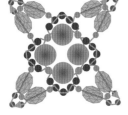

figure 4

figure 5

figure 6

figure 7

Hexagon Components

1 Make a basic bezel (p. 20) using a square in step 1. Use 4mm pearls instead of crystals for the center, 4mm fire-polished beads at the corners, and 12mm crystal rivolis **(figure 1)**.

2 Make a total of three hexagon components.

Cross-Shaped Components

1 Pick up a repeating pattern of an 11º cylinder bead and a 4mm pearl four times, and tie the beads into a ring with a square knot. Sew through the next cylinder, pearl, and cylinder, and pull snug to hide the knot.

2 Pick up five cylinders, skip the pearl, and sew through the following cylinder. Repeat to complete the round. Step up through the center cylinder in a five-bead set **(figure 2)**.

3 Pick up a cylinder, a 4mm fire-polished bead, a cylinder, a fire-polished bead, and a cylinder, and sew through the three center cylinders in the next five-bead set added in the previous round. Repeat to complete the round, and step up through the first cylinder and fire-polished bead **(figure 3)**.

4 Pick up three cylinders, skip the next cylinder, and sew through the next fire-polished bead. Sew through the beadwork to exit the next fire-polished bead. Repeat to complete the round **(figure 4)**. Sew through the beadwork to exit a cylinder in step 1.

5 Repeat step 2 on the back of the component.

6 Pick up two cylinders, and sew through the center cylinder in the next five-bead set added in the previous round. Repeat to complete the round. Retrace the thread path through all the beads just added, pulling tight. End the threads. Make another cross-shaped component.

7 Work as in step 1–6, but in step 1, pick up a repeating pattern of a cylinder and a pearl three times, instead of four. Make a total of two components, referring to **figures 5–7**.

Make the Clasp

1 Make a basic circle (p. 14) using eight pearls and eight fire-polished beads, which serves as the toggle loop. On the back side of the circle (after making the loops of five all around), instead of picking up a fire-polished bead, pick up two or three cylinders.

2 Sew through the beadwork to exit three cylinders. Pick up three cylinders, and sew through the center cylinder in the five-bead set. Repeat to complete the round **(figure 8)**. Retrace the thread path through all the beads in this row to reinforce and pull taut. Set aside.

3 Make a toggle bar (p. 27). Make sure you have at least 2 yd. (1.8m) of thread, as you will assemble the components with this same thread. Sew through the beadwork to exit a cylinder in the center of the tube.

4 Pick up a cylinder, and sew through the top bead of a picot on the end of a triangular component. Pick up a cylinder, and sew through a cylinder in the tube. Retrace the thread path through the join several times to secure. (Repeat this step with the thread tail to link the toggle loop to the other end of the bracelet.) Sew through the beadwork to exit the next top cylinder of a picot in the triangular component.

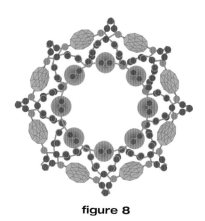

figure 8

Join the Components

1 Pick up a cylinder, a pearl, and a cylinder, and sew through the top cylinder of a picot on the corner of a hexagon component. Sew through the hexagon component to exit a corresponding cylinder on the opposite side of the component.

2 Pick up a cylinder, a pearl, and a cylinder, and sew through the top cylinder of a picot on the corner of a cross-shaped component. Continue joining as shown **(figure 9)**.

3 Once you reach one end, sew through the beadwork to the other side, and work as in steps 1 and 2. End the threads.

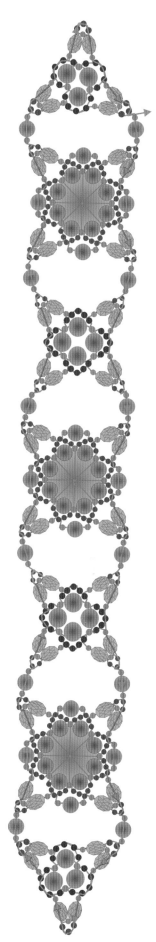

figure 9

Puerto de Luna Necklace

Combine multiple building blocks in this

gorgeous piece. Choose sunlit colors

for a dreamy, watery necklace.

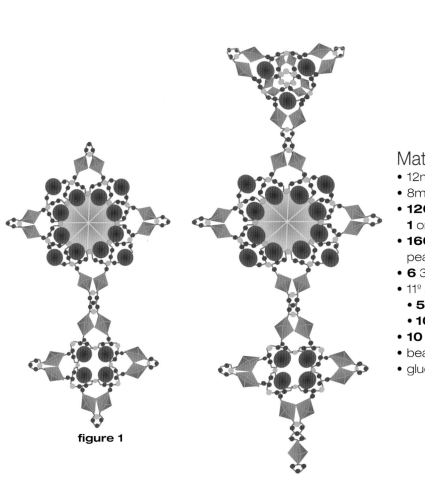

figure 1

figure 2

figure 3

Materials

- 12mm crystal rivoli
- 8mm bicone crystal
- **120–130** 4mm bicone crystals in **1** or **2** colors
- **160–180** 3.5–4mm freshwater pearls
- **6** 3mm crystal bicones, color B
- 11º seed beads
  - **5** grams color A
  - **10** grams color B
- **10** grams 15º seed beads, color B
- beading needle and thread
- glue (optional)

Pendant

1 Make a basic bezel (p. 20) using a square in step 1. Use 4mm pearls, 4mm bicone crystals, color A 11ºs seed beads, and color B 15º seed beads. Refer to **figure 1** to see which beads to use.

2 Make a cross-shaped component from the Bits 'n Pieces Bracelet (p. 59), using pearls, 4mm crystals, A 11ºs, and 15ºs. Refer to **figure 1** to see which pearls, 4mm crystals, and 15ºs to use. When you are adding the picots to the cross-shaped component, join the bezel in the same way as in the Rivoli Revelry Bracelet (p. 48). All joins are done in this manner **(figure 1)**.

3 Exit the center 15º in the picot at the bottom of the cross-shaped component, and pick up a 15º, an 8mm bicone crystal, and three or four 15ºs. Skip the 15ºs, and sew back through the 8mm. Pick up a 15º, and sew back through the 15º your thread exited at the start of this step. Retrace the thread path through the dangle, and sew through the cross-shaped component to exit the center 15º in the picot opposite the dangle (refer to **figure 2**). Reinforce this join by sewing all the way back through all the beads in the dangle. The first two components are complete.

Bail

1 On 1 yd. (.9m) of thread, pick up six color A 11º seed beads, and tie the beads into a ring with a square knot. Sew through the first two beads, and pull tight to hide the knot.

2 Pick up a 15º a 3mm bicone crystal, and a 15º. Skip an A 11º, and sew through the next A 11º. Repeat this step two more times to complete the round, and retrace the thread path in the round. Step up through the next 3mm crystal and 11º **(figure 3)**. (You will do this for each row.) End the short tail.

figure 4

figure 5

figure 6

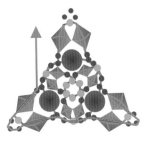

figure 7

3 Pick up two 15⁰s, a pearl, and two 15⁰s. Sew through the A 11⁰ between the next 3mm crystals. Repeat to complete the round, and sew through the next two 15⁰s **(figure 4)**.

4 Pick up a B 11⁰, a 4mm crystal, an A 11⁰, a 4mm crystal, and a B 11⁰. Skip the pearl, and sew through the next two 15⁰s, 11⁰, and two 15⁰s. Repeat two times to complete the round, and step up through the next B 11⁰ and 4mm crystal **(figure 5)**.

5 Pick up three 15⁰s. Skip the next 11⁰, and sew through the next 4mm crystal. Sew through the beadwork to exit the next 4mm crystal **(figure 6)**, and repeat two more times to complete the round **(figure 7)**.

6 Finish the back of the bail (p. 23). Join the bail to the top of the square as in **figure 2**, adding extra 15⁰s for the connection, if necessary.

Spiral Rope

The necklace portion is a spiral rope. Follow the instructions for the basic spiral rope (p. 25). The sequence for this rope is as follows:

1 On 6–7 ft. (1.8–2.13m) of thread, pick up nine 11⁰s: four B 11⁰s (the core beads), a 15⁰, an A 11⁰,

a B 11⁰, an A 11⁰, and a 15⁰. This is Sequence One for the beginning and end of the rope. Sew back through four of the B 11⁰s (the core beads) just picked up.

2 Pick up a B 11⁰, and the sequence of a 15⁰, an A 11⁰, a B 11⁰, an A 11⁰, and a 15⁰, and sew through three of the core beads plus the B 11⁰ just picked up. Repeat Sequence One, and sew through three of the core beads and the first B 11⁰ until your rope is 4 in. (10cm) long.

3 Switch to Sequence Two: a B 11⁰, a 15⁰, an A 11⁰, a pearl, an A 11⁰, and a 15⁰. Sew through three core beads plus the B 11⁰. Repeat Sequence Two three times.

4 Sequence Three is a B 11⁰, a 15⁰, a A 11⁰, a 4mm crystal, an A 11⁰, and a 15⁰. Repeat this sequence once, and then repeat Sequence Two three times. Continue in this manner until you have added 10 4mm crystals.

5 Begin alternating Sequence Three (using a second color of 4mm crystals, if desired) with Sequence Two (pearls) three times. Once the necklace is ½ in. (1.3cm) short of half the desired length, switch back to the initial sequence of all seed beads for about 1 in. (2.5cm). This is where the bail will sit.

6 Slide on the bail, and then reverse the order of the sequences to make the other half of the spiral rope match the first half. When your thread is too short to work with, weave it back up through loops and core beads for a few inches until secure, and cut. Dot with glue, if necessary.

Finish the Necklace

1 Make a toggle clasp (p. 27), using a square for the loop half.

2 Thread your needle with 2 yd. (1.8m) of thread, and sew through about 2 in. (5cm) of core beads and loops. Attach one half of the toggle clasp to each end of the spiral rope.

square,
p. 17

bezel,
p. 20

bail,
p. 23

spiral
rope,
p. 25

Night Blossom Set

Make a bright cuff, pendant, or ring with this

beautiful, highly embellished blossom.

Materials

Medallion
- 12mm crystal rivoli or vintage Czech stone
- 4mm bicone crystals
  - **21** color A
  - **15** color B
- **2** grams 11º seed beads

Ring
- medallion
- **1–2** grams 11º seed beads

Pendant
- medallion
- **9** 4mm bicone crystals for bail
- 18 in. (46cm) chain
- **2** 2-in. (5cm) headpins and a few extra crystals and seed beads for chain (optional)
- roundnose and chainnose pliers (optional)
- wire cutters

Cuff
- medallion
- **18** 4mm bicone crystals
- **12** 3mm bicone crystals
- **3** grams 11º seed beads
- 1 in. (2.5cm) brass cuff blank
- 12 in. (30cm) Ultrasuede, ½ in. (1.3cm) wider than cuff blank
- Crafter's Pick The Ultimate glue and G-S Hypo Cement
- craft knife
- paintbrush

All
- beading needle and thread

Medallion

1 On 1 yd. (.9m) of thread, pick up a color A 4mm bicone crystal, an 11º seed bead, an A, and an 11º until you have six As and six 11ºs. Sew through all the beads again to make a ring, and tie a square knot **(figure 1)**. Sew through the first A and 11º, and pull to hide the knot.

2 Pick up five 11ºs, skip the next A, and sew through the following 11º. Repeat to complete the round, and step up through the first three 11ºs added in this round **(figure 2)**.

3 Pick up an 11º, an A, an 11º, and an A, skip five 11ºs, and sew through the center 11º in the next five-bead set. Pick up an 11º, a color B 4mm bicone crystal, an 11º, a B, and an 11º, skip five 11ºs, and sew through the center 11º in the next five-bead set **(figure 3)**. Repeat these two stitches to complete the round. Retrace the thread path through all the beads in this round to reinforce, exiting a center 11º between a set of As and a set of Bs **(figure 4)**.

4 Pick up five 11ºs, and sew through the center 11º between the next set of As and Bs **(figure 5)**. Repeat to complete the round, and step up through the first three beads added in this round (this is the back of the medallion) **(figure 6)**. End the tail.

5 Insert the rivoli face-down in the center of the medallion, and complete the next row on the back, holding the rivoli in place with your thumb: Pick up two 11ºs, and sew through the center 11º in the next five-bead set added in the previous round. Repeat to complete the round, and then retrace the thread path through all the beads added in this round to reinforce, pulling taut.

6 Turn the medallion over to the front, and sew through the beadwork to exit an 11º between the two 4mms along the outer edge **(figure 7)**. Pick up an A, three 11ºs, and a B, and sew through the 11º between the next two crystals in the previous row. Pick up a B, three 11ºs, and an A, and sew through the 11º between the next two crystals of the previous row. Repeat these two stitches to complete the round. Sew through the beadwork to exit the first A in the next cluster of As **(figure 8)**.

7 Pick up an A and three 11ºs. Skip the 11ºs, and sew back down through the A just added, the next A in the cluster, and the next 11º. Pick up three 11ºs, skip the next 11º in the previous round, and sew through the following 11º and the next B. Pick up a B and three 11ºs, skip the 11ºs, and sew back down through the B, the next B, and the following 11º. Pick up three 11ºs, skip the next 11º in the previous round, and sew through the following 11º and the next A. Repeat this step two more times to complete the round, and end the threads **(figure 9)**.

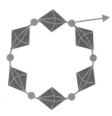

figure 1

figure 2

figure 3

figure 4

figure 5

figure 6

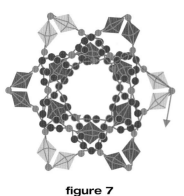

figure 7

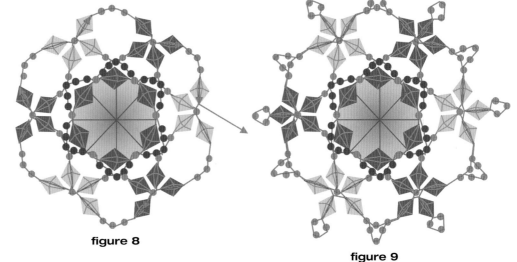

figure 8

figure 9

Ring

1 Create a medallion.

2 Make a piece of flat peyote six beads wide. Make it long enough to fit comfortably around your finger as in the Bling Ring (p. 38). Zip up the ends to make a ring.

3 Use the remaining thread to sew the ring band to the back of the component. Reinforce until secure. End the thread.

Pendant

1 Create a medallion.

2 Make a basic bail (p. 23).

3 Complete the bail and join the pieces: Sew through the beadwork to exit the second bead in a picot on a corner of the front piece of the bail. Pick up an 11º, and sew through the second bead of one of the picots on the square portion of the pendant (see the photo of the piece for construction).

4 Pick up another 11º, and sew through the 11º and 4mm of the bail. Sew all the way around the last row on the bail to reinforce, and make sure to reinforce the join several times. End the thread.

5 String a chain through the bail to the desired length.

6 To add optional crystal links to your chain, cut the chain about 4½ in. (11.4cm) from the clasp on one end. Cut the head off a headpin, and make a plain loop on one end, String an 11º, a 4mm, and an 11º, and make a plain loop on the other end. Open a loop, and attach an end link of the chain to the wire. Close the loop. Attach the other end loop of the link to the remaining long piece of chain.

7 Repeat step 6 to make another crystal link.

Cuff

1 Create a medallion; set aside.

2 Make two triangular components as in the Puerta de Luna Necklace (p. 62), "Bail" steps 1–5. Use A 4mms instead of pearls.

3 To assemble: Cut a strip of Ultrasuede ¼ in. (6mm) wider than your cuff and about 12 in. (30cm) long. Lay it over the front of the cuff and cut it ¼ in. longer than the front of the cuff. Do the same thing with the remaining piece for the inside of the cuff.

4 Find the center of the piece of Ultrasuede for the front of the cuff. Cut a very small diamond shape in the center. (Fold it in half, then lengthwise to find the center, and cut the folded corner.)

5 Place the center of the medallion over the cutout, and stitch the medallion to the Ultrasuede by taking a stitch every so often, connecting the medallion to the Ultrasuede until it is secure. End the threads.

6 Work in the same manner to attach the two triangular components to the Ultrasuede where desired.

7 Use a paintbrush to apply a thin, even layer of Crafter's Pick the Ultimate glue to about one third of the front of your brass blank. Lay the Ultrasuede on the bracelet blank, and smooth it down. Make sure to leave ¼ in. (6mm) on either side and on the ends. Once you have the first third glued, brush on more glue, and continue gluing and smoothing the Ultrasuede. Let it dry for about an hour (while you start your next medallion!).

8 Once the Ultrasuede is dry, apply a thin line of glue on the back along one side. This part can't be rushed. Fold over the excess Ultrasuede to the back, and press down. Be careful not to get any glue on the Ultrasuede. If you do, quickly blot with a damp cloth. Don't rub. Hold the folded edge down until the glue sets. Move your fingers along the side until the edge is nicely folded over to the back of the cuff. Repeat for the other side. Let the glue dry.

9 Once the glue is dry, apply a thin layer of glue to the back of the cuff. Also, carefully apply a line of glue on the folded edges. Lay the remaining piece of Ultrasuede on the glue, position it, and smooth it down. Let it dry. If necessary, you can use G-S Hypo Cement to glue down the edge more.

10 Once it is dry, cut the ends of the pieces of Ultrasuede, following the line of the cuff. Leave about ⅛ in. (3mm) beyond the edge of the cuff. Trim to the shape of the end of the blank, if necessary.

11 Thread a needle with a comfortable length of thread and knot the end. You will now bead an edge stitch on each end of the cuff: Thread your needle with a workable length, and knot the end. Sew through the Ultrasuede, and pick up three 11⁰s.

12 Sew back down through the two Ultrasuede layers, and then sew back up through both layers and the third 11⁰ picked up.

13 Pick up two 11⁰s, and sew down through both layers and back up through the second 11⁰.

14 Continue in this fashion to the other side, joining the two layers. Repeat on the other end of the cuff. Your last stitch will only have one bead on it. If you need to add thread, weave through previous stitches with your old thread until it is secure, and cut. Thread your needle again, and knot. Weave the thread into the appropriate bead to start the edge stitch again, and continue.

15 When finished, knot the thread, dab it with glue, and pull the knot into the beadwork to hide it.

Materials

- **64** 4mm crystal bicones
- **67** 4mm glass pearls
- **5–7** grams 11º seed beads
- beading needle and thread

Pearl Bridges Bracelet

This delicate, yet sturdy, web of pearls and

crystals will enhance any outfit. A beautiful

purple-and-petrol version is fit for a queen!

figure 1

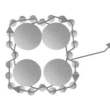

figure 2

figure 3

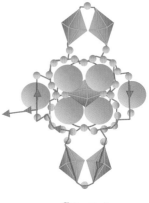

figure 4

Pearl Component

1 Pick up a repeating pattern of an 11º seed bead and a 4mm pearl four times. Sew back through all the beads, and tie the beads into a ring with a square knot **(figure 1)**. Sew through a pearl and an 11º, and pull to hide the knot.

2 Pick up five 11ºs, skip a pearl, and sew through the next 11º. Repeat to complete the round, and sew through the next six 11ºs **(figure 2)**.

3 Pick up an 11º, a 4mm bicone crystal, and an 11º, and sew through the 11º directly across the component as shown in **figure 3**.

4 Sew back through the 11º, crystal, and 11º. Sew through the beadwork to exit the fourth 11º in a five-bead set **(figure 3)**.

5 Pick up an 11º, a crystal, an 11º, a crystal, and an 11º, skip three 11ºs, and sew through the next three 11ºs. Pick up an 11º, a pearl, and an 11º, skip three 11ºs, and sew through the next three 11ºs. Repeat this step one time, sew through the beadwork, and exit an 11º before a pearl in the last round **(figure 4)**.

6 Pick up five 11ºs, skip the next pearl, and sew through the following 11º. Sew through the beadwork to exit the 11º before the pearl on the opposite side and repeat this step. Sew through the beadwork again, and step up through the next 11º between the crystals **(figure 5)**.

7 Pick up a crystal, five 11ºs, a pearl, and an 11º, and sew through the third 11º in the set of five going over the single pearl added in the previous round **(figure 6)**. Pick up an 11º, a pearl, five 11ºs, and a crystal, and sew through the 11º between the next two crystals. Repeat this step to complete the round, exiting the 11º you began with in this step **(figure 7)**.

8 Pick up a crystal and an 11º. Skip the 11º, and sew back down through the crystal and the next crystal and two 11ºs.

9 Pick up three 11ºs, skip an 11º, and sew through two 11ºs, a pearl, and an 11º. Pick up an 11º, skip an 11º, and sew through the next 11º, pearl and two 11ºs **(figure 8)**. Pick up three 11ºs, skip an 11º, and sew through the next two 11ºs and crystal. End the thread.

Put the Pieces Together

1 Begin another pearl component through step 3. End with your thread exiting the fourth 11º in a five-bead set.

2 Pick up a 11º and a crystal, and sew through the 11º at the top of the crystal on one end of the previous medallion (see **figure 9** for crystal attachment).

3 Add picots on the other side of the first medallion as in step 8 of "Pearl Component" **(figure 9)**, and sew back down to the new medallion. Finish the second medallion as in steps 5–9 of "Pearl Component," exiting the center 11º in a three-bead picot.

4 Pick up an 11º, and sew through the second 11º of the picot on the first medallion. Pick up an 11º, and sew back through the first 11º you exited. Retrace the thread path to reinforce.

5 Sew through the beadwork to the other side of one of the medallions, and repeat step 4 **(figure 10)**.

6 Continue to make and join medallions until you have six connected together, and exit an 11º on one end of the bracelet. The bracelet is now 6½ in. (16.5cm) long. With the clasp, it will be a little

figure 5

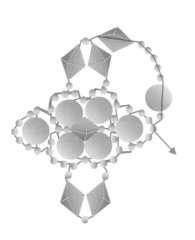

figure 6

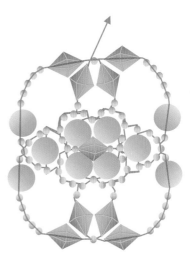

figure 7

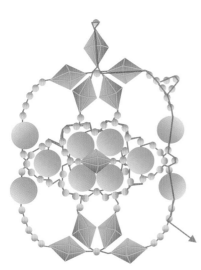

figure 8

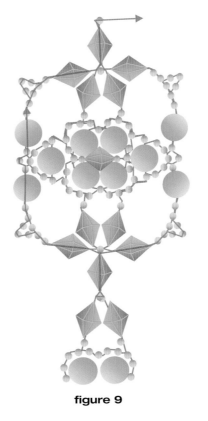

figure 9

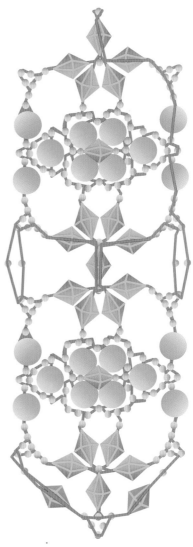

figure 10

over 7 in./18cm. If you need a longer bracelet, add more beads with the toggle bar. If you need an inch or more, make another medallion.

7 Make the loop half of the toggle clasp: With at least 4 ft. (10.2m) of thread on your needle, pick up three 11º's, a pearl, three 11º's, a crystal, three 11º's, a pearl, three 11º's, a crystal, and three 11º's, and sew back through the end 11º you first exited.

8 Pick up three 11º's, skip an 11º, and sew through the next

11º, pearl, and 11º. Pick up three 11º's, and make another picot in the same manner. Continue all the way around the loop, and sew back through the beads to reinforce. End the thread.

9 Make the bar half of a toggle clasp (p. 27), adding a pearl and a picot on one side, and a crystal and a picot on the other side, and attach it to the opposite end of the bracelet.

Night Shine Pendant

Use your favorite colors and create a truly stunning

pendant to showcase a brilliant, embellished square.

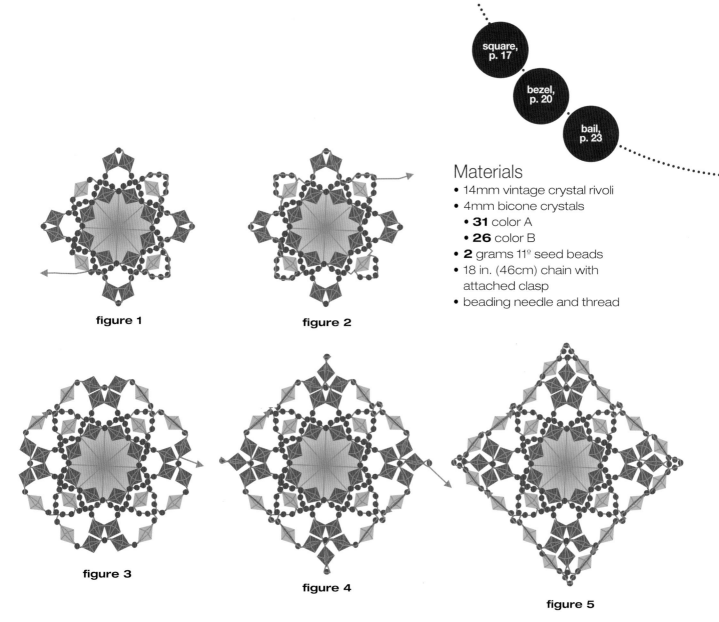

figure 1

figure 2

figure 3

figure 4

figure 5

square, p. 17

bezel, p. 20

bail, p. 23

Materials

- 14mm vintage crystal rivoli
- 4mm bicone crystals
  - **31** color A
  - **26** color B
- **2** grams 11º seed beads
- 18 in. (46cm) chain with attached clasp
- beading needle and thread

Pendant

1 Make a basic bezel (p. 20) using a square in step 1. Use a 14mm rivoli and color A and B 4mm bicone crystals as shown. Exit an 11º seed bead next to a 4mm.

2 Pick up five 11ºs, skip the next 4mm, and sew through the next nine beads to exit the 11º next to the following single 4mm. Repeat **(figure 1)** three more times to complete the round. Sew through the beadwork, and exit the center 11º of the five-bead loop you just created **(figure 2)**.

3 Pick up an 11º, a B, an 11º, and an A, and sew through the 11º between the next two As. Pick up an A, an 11º, a B, and an 11º, and sew through the center 11º of the next five-bead loop from the previous round. Repeat these two stitches three times to complete the round as shown in **figure 3**. Retrace the thread path through the beads added in this round, and exit an A.

4 Pick up an A and an 11º, skip the 11º, and sew back through the A, adjacent A, 11º, B, and 11º. Pick up an 11º, and sew through the next 11º, B, 11º, and A. Repeat these stitches three times to complete the round, and exit the first 11º picked up in this step **(figure 4)**.

5 Pick up an 11º, a B, and an 11º, and sew through the next 11º from the previous round and the beads along the outer edge to exit the 11º before the next A (see **figure 5**). Repeat this step to complete the round, and exit an 11º following a B at one corner of the square.

6 Pick up three 11ºs, skip the next 11º in the previous round, and sew through the beadwork to exit the 11º after the B at the next corner. Continue in this manner to add picots at each corner **(figure 5)**. End the theads.

7 Make a basic bail (p. 23), and join the pendant to the bail as in the Bellagio Pendant (p. 56). Slip the bail on the chain.

Fete de Fee
Necklace

Let out all the stops with a final,

beautiful masterpiece. This necklace makes

me think of faery circles in an evening wood.

Materials

- **2** 14mm crystal rivolis
- **8** 8mm cathedral beads
- **93** 4mm crystal or glass pearls
- **123–130** 4mm bicone crystals
- 11º seed beads
  - **20** grams color A
  - **1** gram color B (for back of pendant, if desired)
- beading needle and thread

figure 1

Pendant

1 Make a Night Shine Pendant (p. 72), using 4mm pearls instead of 4mm bicone crystals where shown and color A 11º seed beads. Exit the middle A 11º in one of the picots on the corner **(figure 1)**.

2 Pick up an 11º, a crystal, and three 11ºs. Sew back down through the crystal, pick up an 11º, and sew through the beadwork to the next corner. With your thread exiting the middle 11º of the next corner picot, repeat to complete the round (you can use a pearl at the top instead of a crystal, if desired). End the threads **(figure 2)**.

Finish the Center

1 Make a triangular component following the instructions for the front of a bail (p. 23), using crystals in the middle and pearls on the outside **(figure 3)**. Once this component is finished, sew through the beadwork to exit the second 11º of a picot on a corner.

2 Connect the pendant and the triangular component as in the Venezia Pendant (p. 54), steps 5 and 6. End the threads **(figure 4)**.

figure 2

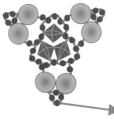

figure 3

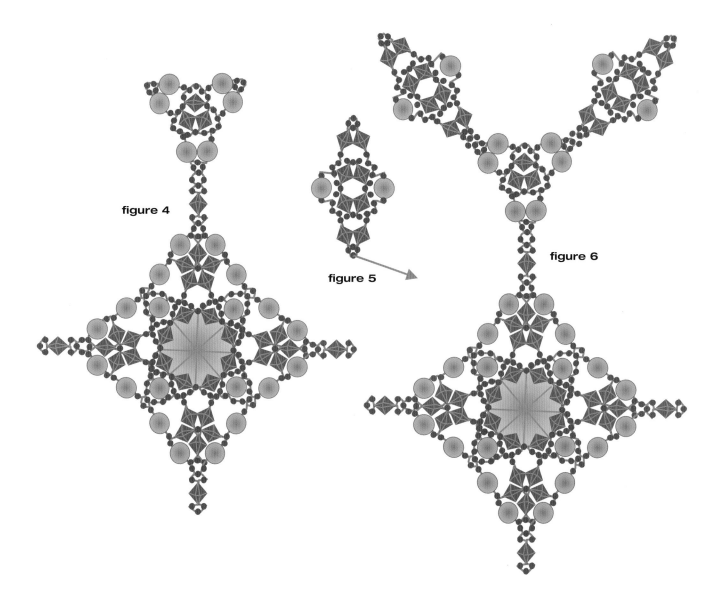

figure 4

figure 5

figure 6

3 Follow the instructions for the Arabesque Bracelet, "Bracelet" steps 1–4 (p. 50), to make an Arabesque component. Start with four sets of crystals and 11⁰s **(figure 5)**. Join the Arabesque component to one of the corners on the triangular component as in step 2. Make a second Arabesque component, and attach it to the other side of the triangular component **(figure 6)**. Make six more Arabesque components, and set aside.

4 Make a basic circle (p. 11) for the center: Start with eight sets of crystals and 11⁰s, and follow step 2 to make the loops of five 11⁰s all around.

5 With the thread exiting the third 11⁰ in a five-bead loop, pick up an 11⁰, and sew through a pearl on the side of one Arabesque component. Pick up an 11⁰, and sew through the third 11⁰ in the next five-bead loop. Pick up two more pearls in the usual fashion, and then connect the side of the

circle to the other Arabesque component as shown in **figure 7**.

6 Set the rivoli face down in the circle, and complete the bezel (p. 20). Sew through the beadwork to exit an 11⁰ next to a pearl as shown in **figure 7**. Pick up a 4mm crystal and three 11⁰s. Sew back down through the 4mm crystal, skip an 11⁰ in the last round, and sew through the next 11⁰, 4mm crystal, and 11⁰. Repeat this stitch three more times to complete the centerpiece.

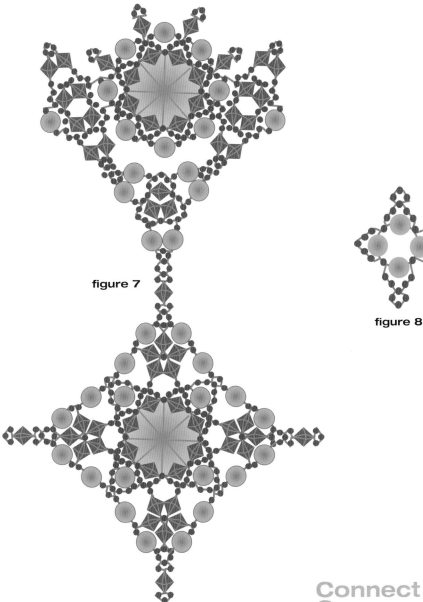

figure 7

figure 8

Pearl Components

The next component is made with pearls as shown in **figure 8**. You will join this component to the top of one of the previous components.

1 Pick up a repeating pattern of an 11º and a pearl four times, and exit an 11º. Pick up five 11ºs, skip a pearl, and sew through the next 11º. Repeat to complete the round, and step up through the first three 11ºs added in this round, Pick up three 11ºs, and sew back through the 11º you just exited and the next 12 11ºs. Pick up three 11ºs, and sew back through the 11º you just exited **(figure 8)**. If desired,

sew through the beadwork to an 11º between two pearls, pick up a 4mm crystal, and sew through the opposite 11º between the two pearls, placing the crystal on the back of the component to add a bit of see-through sparkle.

2 Make six pearl components. Join a pearl component to the necklace: Pick up an 11º, and sew through the second bead of the three-bead picot of the previous Arabesque component. Reinforce the join a couple of times, and end the thread.

Connect the Components

1 Exit the top 11º on the picot of the pearl component, and sew through the second 11º in a three-bead picot on an Arabesque component. Retrace the thread path, and sew through the beadwork to exit the top 11º of the three-bead picot on the Arabeque component. Pick up an 11º, a pearl, a cathedral bead, a pearl, and an 11º, and sew through the second 11º in a three-bead picot on a pearl component. Pick up an 11º, sew back down through the pearl, cathedral bead, and pearl, and pick up an 11º. Sew through the first 11º you exited, and continue through the beadwork to exit the top 11º of the three-bead picot on the pearl component.

2 From this point, alternate Arabesque components with pearl components, separated by an 11º, a pearl, a cathedral bead, a pearl, and an 11º. You will have a total of three pearl and three Arabesque components. Repeat on the other side of the necklace.

Finish the Piece

1 Once both sides of the necklace are complete, make a toggle clasp using a circle in step 1 (p. 27). Use eight sets of crystals in the center, and use pearls on the outer ring. Make a bar using pearls instead of crystals, with a three-bead picot on each end. Attach the toggle loop to one end of the necklace: Exit a pearl, pick up three 11ºs, and sew through the top bead of a three-bead picot on the end

of the necklace. Sew back through the last 11º, pick up two 11ºs, and sew through the pearl again. Retrace the thread path through the join several times to secure, and end the thread.

2 Attach the toggle bar to the other end of the necklace: Pick up an 11º, and sew through the top bead of a three-bead picot on the end of the necklace. Pick up an 11º, and sew back through an 11º on the tube. Retrace the thread path through the join several times to secure, and end the threads.

About the Author

Beading since birth (relatively speaking), creating is as natural to Nikia as breathing—and just as necessary. Nikia Angel has been beading since she was a child, and obsessively since 1988. She is owner of Stone Mountain Bead Gallery, and is constantly working to come up with new and innovative designs to share with her fellow beaders.

Teaching since 1990, Nikia has instructed at many major bead and jewelry shows, as well as bead stores, across the country. She enjoys sharing her passion and love for all things beady, and inspiring students of all ages to share her love of jewelry making.

When she isn't busy beading or traveling the country, Nikia resides in Albuquerque, N.M. Contact her at http://www.etsy.com/shop/Nikia.

Explore countless ways to create with crystals!

Endless Sparkle
12 crystal components · unlimited jewelry designs

Aimee Carpenter

Learn how to fashion 12 easy, eye-catching crystal components and then turn these sparkly bits into charming rings, pendants, earrings, and necklaces.

64223 • $19.95

Crystal *Brilliance*

Making designer jewelry with crystal beads

CREATE YOUR STYLE with CRYSTALLIZED™ – Swarovski Elements

Anna Elizabeth Draeger

Whether your style is romantic, geometric, organic, or classic, crystals shine front and center in these glamorous jewelry projects from Anna Elizabeth Draeger.

62953 • $21.95

KALMBACH BOOKS

Buy now from your favorite bead or craft shop!
Or at **www.KalmbachStore.com**
or **1-800-533-6644**
Monday – Friday, 8:30 a.m. – 4:30 p.m. CST.
Outside the United States and Canada call
262-796-8776, ext. 661.

 www.facebook.com/KalmbachJewelryBooks

 www.pinterest.com/kalmbachjewelry

P17990